W9-BBY-909

Amy Pearl

MANOUSH ZOMORODI is the creator of WNYC's podcast *Note to Self* and the cofounder of Stable Genius Productions, a media company with a mission to help people navigate personal and global change. StableG uses podcasts as a lab to test new ways journalists can educate, entertain, and inspire through narrative. Investigating how technology is transforming humanity is Manoush's passion and expertise.

Bored and
Brilliant

Manoush Zomorodi

Bored and Brilliant

———

HOW SPACING OUT CAN UNLOCK YOUR MOST PRODUCTIVE AND CREATIVE SELF

PICADOR ST. MARTIN'S PRESS NEW YORK

BORED AND BRILLIANT. Copyright © 2017 by New York Public Radio. All rights reserved. Printed in the United States of America. For information, address Picador, 175 Fifth Avenue, New York, N.Y. 10010.

picadorusa.com • instagram.com/picador
twitter.com/picadorusa • facebook.com/picadorusa

Picador® is a U.S. registered trademark and is used by Macmillan Publishing Group, LLC, under license from Pan Books Limited.

For book club information, please visit facebook.com/picadorbookclub or email marketing@picadorusa.com.

The Library of Congress has cataloged the St. Martin's Press edition as follows:

Names: Zomorodi, Manoush, author.
Title: Bored and brilliant : how spacing out can unlock your most
    productive and creative self / Manoush Zomorodi.
Description: First edition. | New York : St. Martins Press, [2017]
Identifiers: LCCN 2017017719 | ISBN 9781250124951 (hardcover) |
    ISBN 9781250124968 (ebook)
Subjects: LCSH: Boredom. | Creative ability. | Labor productivity.
Classification: LCC BF575.B67 Z66 2017 | 153.3—dc23
LC record available at https://lccn.loc.gov/2017017719

Picador Paperback ISBN 978-1-250-12665-8

Our books may be purchased in bulk for promotional, educational, or business use. Please contact your local bookseller or the Macmillan Corporate and Premium Sales Department at 1-800-221-7945, extension 5442, or by email at MacmillanSpecialMarkets@macmillan.com.

First published by St. Martin's Press

First Picador Edition: September 2018

10 9 8 7 6 5 4

Kai and Soraya, without you, I never would have known that boredom could lead to brilliance. You are my two sparkles.

Rebecca Paley, you are the ultimate efficient, clear, and creative collaborator. I've admired you since our lives first started intersecting over twenty years ago. Working with you was an organizational and intellectual pleasure. Plus, fun. Thank you.

CONTENTS

Bored and Brilliant

The Case for Boredom

My son and the iPhone were born three weeks apart, in June 2007. I'm more of a 2.0 kind of woman, so I didn't rush out to buy one, and anyway, I had more pressing things to tend to. My new baby was colicky and miserable. I spent hours pushing him around, trying to soothe him to sleep, which he would do only when his stroller was in motion. We probably wandered the equivalent of ten to fifteen miles a day. Our walks were also very quiet because my newborn required utter silence to snooze longer than fifteen minutes at a time, so I couldn't talk on my flip phone or get coffee from the bodega or even just sit on a bench. The baby weight flew off, but I was the most bored I had ever been in my entire life.

At first I was angry, frustrated, and sad. It was the classic story of my generation: A woman goes from urban professional to cloistered mom in one shocking instant. Once upon a time, I was a foreign news producer always dropping into emergency situations no matter where in the world they happened. If the Concorde crashed or the parliament in Belgrade was set on fire, I went. For twelve years I worked in the fast-paced world of broadcast journalism. On my time off, I thought nothing of spending an entire Sunday on the couch to plow through *The New York Times* and the latest novel.

When I became pregnant with my first child, I pictured my husband, Josh, a fellow journalist and adventurer, and me putting the baby in a backpack or something as we traveled the world and were still amazing at our jobs. What a joke. I had no idea. After I had my son, Kai, my ass got kicked so hard. I felt lonely and truly fatigued as never before. *New York Times*? The latest novel? *Us Weekly* was the most I could handle between back-to-back nursing sessions and unloading the dishwasher.

After a few weeks of my stroller-pushing marathons, though, there was a shift. Not only did I get into a rhythm, but I also began to see things around my neighborhood that I'd never noticed before. Ornamental cornices and gargoyles became familiar friends. I grew to be an expert in the blooming patterns of the neighborhood's landscaping. I even knew the cracks and bumps in the sidewalk by heart. I gave in to the discomfort of nonstop walking and started appreciating the fact that I had no destination. (How many times when I was stuck in the office till all hours of the night would I have given anything to roam aimlessly?) Most important, I came to understand what it means to have symbiosis with your child. Being fully in tune with this beautiful new human being I had created required slowing down to a pace that at first made me feel deeply uncomfortable, then completely transformed me.

Indeed, he grew less and less colicky, and soon enough those days of wandering that had soothed both of us ended. I went back to work and, if I'd thought life was busy before, I didn't know the meaning of the word. The next several years flew by in a flurry of personal and professional creativity and effort. I covered tech and business for Reuters, and then New York's public radio station, WNYC; wrote my first book (a guide to making video for nonprofits and businesses); and welcomed a daughter, Soraya.

Then in 2013—after six months of doing weekly news updates on technology after suggesting WNYC cover more of the sector's burgeoning scene in New York—I was offered my dream job, hosting my own weekly radio show and podcast about the human side of technology.

Running the show, which would eventually be called *Note to Self*, I was riding high on possibility. I had the chance to produce something meaningful and interesting about a subject essential to modern life for an intensely responsive group of listeners. This was the opportunity of a lifetime, with creative control and responsibility on a level that I had never experienced before. And if I screwed it up, might never again.

At the start, I was firing on all cylinders. Surrounded by smart, insightful people, I found no shortage of fascinating stories to cover and received great feedback from the public.

Then I hit a wall. Crashed, is more like it. This was different from writer's block, which in the past I'd experienced as a stuck place I needed to work through. This was a blankness. There was just . . . nothing. It was bad.

Part of the problem was, of course, the pressure that came with the unbelievable opportunity before me. Wanting to do the best job possible can be crippling. But there was also something else going on.

My mind felt tired. Worn-out. Why? Yes, I was juggling motherhood, marriage, and career in one of the most hectic cities in the world. But it was more than that. In order to analyze what was going on with me, I began by observing my own behavior. What I found was, frankly, exhausting. As soon as I took a moment to reflect, I realized there wasn't a single waking moment in my life that I didn't find a way to fill—and my main accomplice was my phone.

I had long ago traded in my old flip phone for a smartphone, and now it seemed I spent every spare minute on it. Whether waiting for the subway, in line for coffee, or at my son's preschool for pickup, I was engaged in some kind of information call-and-response. I checked the weather, updated Twitter, responded to e-mails. When I flopped into bed at the end of an exhausting day, instead of turning out the lights, I chose to fire up *Two Dots*—a game that I couldn't stop playing despite myself. I wasn't using my smartphone to connect. I was using it to escape. Scrolling through Twitter made my long commute disappear. Updating my calendar obsessively gave me the feeling of productivity. As my life ramped up, so had the pace and quantity of my technology consumption. My brain was always occupied, but my mind wasn't doing anything with all the information coming in.

In trying to figure out when, in the past, my best ideas had come to me, I was reminded of my time with Kai. During those long, solitary, tech-free walks, where I was cataloguing the details of everything I saw around me, I also did an internal assessment of the professional skills I'd acquired over the previous fifteen years. Like my meandering strolls, it wasn't a conscious accounting but rather a winding mental trip through my career so far and how I might like to put my skills to work next. I let my mind go. It went to some dark and uncomfortable places, but it also went to some weird and wonderful ones.

Looking back at that experience during this hectic period of my life, I saw a connection between a lack of stimulation—boredom—and a flourishing of creativity and drive. It was so clear to me because the cycle of technological innovation sped up at exactly the same time my life did, too. Between the time my son was born and could walk, we saw mobile technology change the way people called a taxi, ordered food, found a date. Suddenly, very basic societal actions that had remained unchanged for decades were upended. And then, when the next operating system came out six months later, upended again. My life wasn't just pre-children and post-children . . . it was simultaneously pre–mobile phone, post–mobile phone. Both children and smartphones shifted me to the core.

In light of all this, I asked myself, "Can my lack of ideas have to do with never being bored?"

The Original Bored and Brilliant Project

There is no question that we are at an unprecedented point in history, where our attention is in hot demand. With the advent of smartphones and tablets, mobile consumers now spend an average of two hours and fifty-seven minutes each day on mobile devices and about eleven hours a day in front of a screen. Although we don't know if all this screen time will have longer-term harmful effects, we know technology is changing us (and it's unclear whether it's for the better).

Parents fret about how to raise healthy and confident children in the digital age. If our children are constantly engaged with bits and bytes of information, what is happening to their ability to imagine, concentrate deeply, reflect on past experiences, decide how to apply those lessons to future goals, and figure out what they want for themselves, their relationships, and life?

It isn't just parents who worry about the shift in how we use our brains in the tech age. The implications for business are significant as well. There is evidence that people could be better at their jobs if they weren't always plugged in. The Bank of England's chief economist said he fears that skills building, innovation, and entire economies could be at risk because "fast thought could make for slow growth."

And what does all this scrolling, processing, blue light, and more mean for our health? All you have to do is stay up hours past your bedtime, playing *Two Dots* (as I shamefully have), to know the answer—sometimes it's relaxing, but most of the time, not so much.

With so many big questions stemming from my central quandary, I dived into trying to understand what happens when we constantly keep our brains busy and never give ourselves time to mentally meander. I spoke with neuroscientists and cognitive psychologists about "mind-wandering"—what our brains do when we're doing nothing at all, or not fully focused on a task.

We may feel like we are doing very little when we endlessly fold laundry, but our brains are actually hard at work. When our minds wander, we activate something called the "default mode," the mental place where we solve problems and generate our best ideas, and engage in what's known as "autobiographical planning," which is how we make sense of our world and our lives and set future goals. The default mode is also involved in how we try to understand and empathize with other people, and make moral judgments.

When we let ourselves space out and our minds wander, we do our most original thinking and problem solving; without distraction, your mind can go to some interesting and unexpected places. Creativity—no matter how you define or apply it—needs a push, and boredom, which allows new and different connections to form in our brain, is a most effective muse. It's what the futurist Rita King calls "the tedium of creativity."

For King—someone whose job it is to conceive of anything from how a town might look two hundred years from now to actions business leaders should embark on to take advantage of trends coming down the line—creativity is her business. "The mistake a lot of people make is to assume the euphoria of an idea is going to persist all the way through the countless little steps that need to happen before the idea becomes real," she says. "Many lose heart or momentum because those little tiny things that have to get done are so dull." The tedium of creativity can be daunting, King explains, especially when compared to the satisfaction of crossing things off a to-do list—which explains why I make my to-do list so long.

But if we let it, inspiration can strike if we give ourselves permission to take time to focus on nothing in particular—before drifting off to sleep, in the shower, while taking a walk in the woods. The default mode is not surprisingly also called the "imagination network." Being bored gives us the space to ask "What if?" That's an essential question regarding not only any creative endeavor but also our emotional health and personal growth.

According to Dr. Jonathan Smallwood, professor of cognitive neuroscience and an expert in mind-wandering at the University of York, "In a very deep way, there's a close link between originality and creativity and the spontaneous thoughts we generate when our minds are idle." In other words, you have to let yourself be bored to be brilliant.

So, I wanted to know: if we changed our relationship to our gadgets, could we generate bigger and better ideas? Would there be a ripple effect of changes to the way we work, the way we parent, the way we relate to one another? Could this change the way we see the world? Suspecting *Note to Self* listeners would want to know as well, in February 2015, my team and I created the Bored and Brilliant Project to investigate and test my theory. We developed a weeklong series of challenges designed to help people detach from their devices and jump-start their creativity.

I heard a lot of listeners and people around me grumbling that everyone these days is "always looking at their phone." But I wasn't sure if rethinking our relationship to smartphones, laptops, and tablets would spark a lot of enthusiasm from the public. My bosses at WNYC, however, told me to trust my instincts. So I put aside my doubts and asked others to join me in reclaiming time to "space out." And listeners of all ages vigorously nodded *Yes!* They showed their support with tweets and e-mails and Facebook posts (ironic, I know)—and, most important, by signing up for the project.

In the end, more than twenty thousand people signed on to the Bored and Brilliant Project, from just about every state. (The highest concentrations of participants were from New York City, San Francisco, L.A., D.C., Chicago, and—out of the blue—Arkansas.) We also had participants from Slovakia, Israel, Denmark, Australia, and the UK. This was something a lot of people had been thinking about, even though the problem hadn't yet been *named*.

Before we began, we surveyed the participants on their motivations, desires, and dreams for this experiment. From the answers we received, a few clear trends and themes emerged. *Forty percent* of them said that they wanted to cut down on the constant checking of their phones and override this newly developed, all-encompassing instinct. Some wanted to model better behavior for their children, who are keenly aware every time their parents' eyes dart toward a screen or their thumbs start texting. Others yearned to figure out the line between "wasting time" and "valuable networking" on social media sites like Facebook and Twitter. Then there were people who appreciated the ability afforded them by technology to stay connected but wished to set boundaries so that they couldn't be reached *all the time*.

The top three concerns we heard were the following:

It's messing with my productivity
I feel addicted
It might actually be affecting my health

Those were my concerns as well. But is there any data to support our suspicions? According to experts in boredom, such as Dr. Sandi Mann from the University of Central Lancashire, we're onto something. Cell phones and other mobile tech devices surely affect our brains, but we're only beginning to get research confirming that. And any evidence that does exist is circumstantial at best. There are no random control studies comparing people with cell phones in their lives to those without. We are all doing our own grand experiment, but we may not know the results until we've experienced the consequences, good and bad.

We really don't know what long-term effects smartphones may have. There's disagreement about whether we're using technology to achieve our goals, or our brains are adapting to use technology more efficiently. Similarly, the scientific research into the phenomenon of mind-wandering is also in its infancy. Still, studies suggest that to think original thoughts, we must put a stop to constant stimulation.

It's not hyperbole to say that we are at a crossroads in the human condition. Different thinkers have called this period the Information Age or the Intelligence Era. Production is no longer measured in physical quantities as it was in the Industrial Age but by data and other intangible elements. Rita King defines our times as the "Imagination Age," because imagination allows us to make connections between the intangibles that drive our culture and society. If true, it's more crucial than ever that we give our brains the break they need to stoke ingenuity.

My Phone, How Do I Love Thee? Let Me Count the Ways . . .

My laptop, tablet, and phone know me better than anyone or anything else. They know what I like and how to grab my attention. Hell, they even know all my passwords. Here's how other Bored and Brilliant participants described their relationships to their phones:

> "The relationship between a baby and its teddy bear or a baby and a binky or a baby that wants its mother's cradle when it's done being held by a stranger . . . that's the relationship between me and my phone."
>
> —Ron

"I think I treat my phone as sort of this friend, like a best friend, who has all of the best and worst qualities, but if I'm sort of passive, and let this friend take the reins, then they'll run away with me and distract me and make my life crazy."

—William

"I feel like I stare at screens all day long, and not only is it unhealthy, but antisocial. Sometimes it feels like the attention I give to my phone prevents me from experiencing the world around me. It is so strange to look up on the train and realize that most everyone is staring into a screen. It's dystopian. I want to escape!"

—Sandra

"Useful but dangerous if not handled properly."

—Anne

After the week of challenges for the Bored and Brilliant Project ended, we did another survey to see if and how people's behavior had changed over the trial period. I'll admit I was disappointed that collectively we shaved off six minutes of phone use for the week. But MIT technology and society professor Sherry Turkle, author of the critically acclaimed *Reclaiming Conversation: The Power of Talk in a Digital Age*, said of the project, "The greater result was not just behavior change, but people feeling that they had a way to reflect on their own behavior, on what they were doing; we want to start a conversation to find ways forward."

Indeed, people told us they felt they had been fundamentally changed by the experience. Seventy percent of them reported that after the experimental week, they felt as though they had enough time to think. "It's like I'm awakening from an extended mental hibernation," one person said. Writers finally finished their manuscripts, entrepreneurs solved those knotty problems at work, teachers had more eye contact with students in class. In control of how and how much time they spent with their phones, tablets, and computers, people were more productive and creative. Word of the project spread like wildfire. High schools asked for curriculum plans; corporations wanted entire departments to do the project together; freshmen at the University of New Orleans requested that every semester kick off with a Bored and Brilliant week.

How We Got Here

The Bored and Brilliant series we aired on *Note to Self* was over, but the larger project was just getting started. I was still curious. I knew I had only scratched the surface of boredom. Why does boredom have such a bad rap? Is our fear of being bored an instinct, or a cultural construct? What really happens in our brains when we're bored? To our kids' brains? And if business puts a premium on original thought, what happens when we don't give our brains the chance to think? There was so much more to our changing relationship with our gadgets.

The result of my obsession with boredom is this book: an exploration of the history, cultural issues, and science of being bored, guided by studies, stories, and conversations with researchers, doctors, artists, and ordinary people. I also refined the original action program that was so successful with my listeners in getting them to reclaim control over their tech lives. The outcome is a seven-step plan that harnesses boredom's hidden benefits so that we can discover our own personal brilliance.

I want to be clear—this book is *not* anti-tech. Computers, the Internet, and mobile devices connect us and make us more informed and knowledgeable. Thanks to all this connectivity, I can work full-time and actually see my two kids. I am profoundly grateful for that, and I'm not longing for a simpler time when we all used pay phones. (Remember those?)

Whenever society acquires a new technological skill or ability, there's an unsettling period during which we're besotted with the technology, using it indiscriminately without really understanding its effects. While swearing off our devices isn't necessarily the solution, for many of us the honeymoon phase with our gadgets is decidedly over.

"What we need is to support people in thinking about how they can integrate these technologies most usefully and most advantageously into our daily lives," says Dr. Mary Helen Immordino-Yang, associate professor of education, psychology, and neuroscience at the University of Southern California's Brain and Creativity Institute. "We need to learn how to manage these online worlds so that they can be advantageously utilized but don't interfere with our greater potential. We need to figure out how to best leverage and adaptively use them."

We need to step back and say, "Hey, look at where our phones and tablets are taking us, and is that where we want to go?" Social connection is great, but not at the price of disconnecting from yourself. Becoming strategic about how we integrate these devices into our lives in ways that promote true social understanding and creativity begins with admitting their true impact on us. Once we take a good hard look at our behavior, we can then be purposeful and manage that impact. By better understanding how our devices and our brains compute differently, we regular folks can also advocate for ourselves within the tech industry by putting pressure on its leaders to make digital tools that improve our lives—and not just give us more to do.

From all my research, one thing is clear: We crave reflective time; we seek balance; we want a life full of joy and curiosity. That's what the Bored and Brilliant Project is all about. A personal guide that anyone can access, this is a tool for teaching digital self-regulation and living a more conscious online existence.

How to Use This Book

When we ran the first Bored and Brilliant experiment, I didn't think people would want me to dictate exactly how they should modify their behavior. Rather, I assumed they would prefer ideas and assignments they could tailor to their own needs. I was wrong. Most really wanted specific tasks with details so they could understand if they were completing them correctly. I'll admit, at the time I wasn't sure what was right, incorrect, or half done when it came to these challenges. But now, having tested out all the steps and having made tweaks based on feedback from that first large group of Bored and Brilliant participants, I have codified the program into a series of effective and clear steps. (I still encourage you to make personal adjustments wherever you see fit.)

There are seven challenges in the Bored and Brilliant program, and they come at the end of every chapter in the book (starting with chapter 2). Designed to build your capacity for boredom, they lead you step-by-step through an understanding of your relationship to your technology and where our brains and technology can conflict. We'll experiment with different methods to help you create more mental space and engage in deeper and more productive thinking and, finally, help you jump-start your creativity and push you to think on a deeper level.

I suggest reading the book from start to finish without doing the challenges, so you can read at your own pace and absorb material. Once you are done, find a week (but don't wait too long) in which you can commit to doing the challenges sequentially, one a day. If you want to keep a challenge (or two, or all of them) going for more than a day, great!

You can expect to find certain challenge days far easier than others. Some will come naturally, while others will make you squirm. Whatever happens, I can promise you'll be changed (even if only in a small, six-minutes-off-your-daily-phone-use way). As one high-level HR media executive wrote to me after he participated in the original weeklong challenge, "I went in quite a bit skeptical, but you converted me. I'm always on the prowl for new ways of thinking and new ways of doing things. It was very different, but well worth my time."

The Bored and Brilliant Project works as an eye-opening activity on both an individual and group level. Consider recruiting family, friends, or colleagues to do the challenges with you. In the end, no matter why or how you do Bored and Brilliant, remember that the goal is to create more curiosity, creativity, and joy in your life. So don't be too hard on or rigid with yourself. Simply go through the steps and let things unfold.

A Quick Word About Creativity and Defining Brilliance

What constitutes "creative thinking"? Your ideas don't have to be life changing in order to be creative. Maybe for you it's finding a way to help your kid cope with math exams or better configuring your furniture to the awkward shape of your living room. My previous goals have been coming up with new show ideas and figuring out how to help my son make friends at camp. Whatever comes to mind, let's agree it's more useful than getting to another level of *Candy Crush*. As for brilliance, we aren't aiming for Stephen Hawking–level smarts, just making space to be our best cognitive selves.

The Bored and Brilliant Seven-Step Program

CHALLENGE ONE: Observe Yourself
First you'll track your digital habits—and most likely be shocked by what you discover.

CHALLENGE TWO: Keep Your Devices Out of Reach While in Motion
Keep your phone out of sight while you're in transit—so no walking and texting!

CHALLENGE THREE: Photo-Free Day
No pics of food, kitten, kids—nada.

CHALLENGE FOUR: Delete That App
Take the one app you can't live without and trash it. (Don't worry, you'll live.)

CHALLENGE FIVE: Take a Fakecation
You'll be in the office but out of touch.

CHALLENGE SIX: Observe Something Else
Reclaim the art of noticing.

CHALLENGE SEVEN: The Bored and Brilliant Challenge
In a culmination of all the exercises, you'll use your new powers of boredom to make sense of your life and set goals.

1

What We Talk About
When We Talk About
Boredom

I like boring things.

—Andy Warhol

Teenagers whine about it constantly. Office mates step out multiple times a day to Starbucks to escape it. Parents die of it every night as they try to get small children to fall asleep. We use the word "boring" so often these days, it's hard to believe it appeared for the first time relatively recently, in 1853, in the Charles Dickens novel *Bleak House*. While some historians believe the term "boredom" emerged as a response to the Industrial Revolution (when people in the Western world, who were becoming less religious, had more free time—including more time to feel, yes, bored), it's only common sense to presume that the feeling has existed since the dawn of man. (Well, maybe cavemen who lived in fear of everything didn't get bored.) As one of my listeners, Deacon Michael G. Hackett of the Episcopal Diocese of Louisiana, told me, boredom "has been around since the desert fathers, who lived as hermits, and were very often bored in their caves."

Just because the word doesn't appear in writing until the Industrial Revolution doesn't mean people throughout the ages weren't "bored";

they just used different terminology to describe the same sensation. Depression. Existential crisis. Nausea (also the title of Jean-Paul Sartre's 1938 novel about philosophical boredom and my favorite book in high school—not sure what that says about me).

The neuroscience age, in which we are only beginning to really get to know our brains, is redefining boredom all over again in exciting and positive new ways. That's where we'll spend most of our investigation. But before we dive into contemporary concepts of this murky and magical world, it will be helpful to take a trip back in time.

A Very Brief History of Boredom

"A rose by any other name would smell as sweet," and boredom by any other name is, well, just as boring. Whatever terminology they used, linguists, writers, and thinkers throughout the ages have grappled with the idea of boredom. My guide to the history of boredom was Peter Toohey, a classics professor at the University of Calgary, who curiously became interested in the topic because it is totally absent in the ancient world. "It always struck me as such a conundrum that the Greeks, Romans, and parallel cultures never talk about boredom," Toohey says. "They see it as so trivial, it's hardly worth mentioning."

Toohey's initial interest grew into an entire book, *Boredom: A Lively History*, which firmly places boredom in those ancient cultures through examples both high (Seneca describing boredom as nausea or sickness) and low (graffiti found in Pompeii that says in Latin, "Wall! I wonder that you haven't fallen down in ruin, when you have to support all the boredom of your inscribers"). Latin *taedia* turned into the Christian *acedia*, the "noonday demon" of listlessness and restlessness, which became the full-blown sin *melancholia* during the Renaissance only to mellow out later into the French idea of *ennui*.

The German philosopher Arthur Schopenhauer described the emotion as "a tame longing without any particular object," while Søren Kierkegaard, who preferred the word "idle" to "bored," believed it was a central state of being in that "everyone who lacks a sense of it thereby shows that he has not raised himself to the human level."

"There are lots of ways of saying you're bored," Toohey sums up.

In contemporary thought, the German psychologist Martin Doehle-mann divided "situational boredom" from "existential boredom," a distinction picked up by the Norwegian historian-philosopher Lars Svendsen in his seminal book *A Philosophy of Boredom*. For both thinkers, situational or simple boredom describes the mild sensation produced by temporarily unavoidable and predictable circumstances such as a long road trip or dull dinner party talk. It's manageable, because you know it'll eventually come to an end.

The other kind of boredom is the existential and spiritual kind—a powerful and unrelieved sense of emptiness, isolation, and alienation. Like depression but different. Toohey, however, explained how the soul-crushing variety of boredom has been embraced by philosophers like Martin Heidegger, who believed it a necessary process leading one to a deeper understanding of the world and one's place in it.

I don't know about that, but the acute discomfort of the latter kind of boredom certainly helped explain its current bad rap. When I first told friends, family, and coworkers about my plan to rediscover boredom, they looked at me as though I were crazy. As my friend Maria Popova—the creator of the influential Web site *Brain Pickings*, an ongoing compendium of thought-provoking material drawn from a wide variety of subjects and sources—said, "We treat boredom as Ebola, something to be eradicated."

Even *Note to Self* listeners were put off by the idea. Why not just call it "daydreaming" or something else that sounded more positive, many wrote me. Some seemed angry that I insisted on referring to boredom as such. I tried to explain that the sensation I was missing wasn't actually fun. It made me feel uncomfortable, or slightly disgusted, as Toohey put it. To separate that yucky feeling from the magic that it could lead to seemed disingenuous to me. No, I wanted to bring back "boredom" in every one of its multifaceted and confusing aspects . . . along with my tolerance for it. I think Kierkegaard and Heidegger would approve.

"Every emotion has a purpose—an evolutionary benefit," says Dr. Sandi Mann, a psychologist and the author of *The Upside of Downtime: Why Boredom Is Good*. "I wanted to know why we have this emotion of boredom, which seems like such a negative, pointless emotion."

That's how Mann got started in her specialty: boredom. While researching emotions in the workplace in the 1990s, she discovered the second most commonly suppressed emotion after anger was—you guessed it—boredom. "It gets such bad press," she said. "Almost everything seems to be blamed on boredom."

As Mann dived into the topic of boredom, she found that it was actually "very interesting." It's certainly not pointless. Dr. Wijnand van Tilburg from the University of Southampton explained the important evolutionary function of that uneasy, awful feeling this way: "Boredom makes people keen to engage in activities that they find more meaningful than those at hand."

"Imagine a world where we didn't get bored," Mann said. "We'd be perpetually excited by everything—raindrops falling, the cornflakes at breakfast time." Once past boredom's evolutionary purpose, Mann became curious about whether there might be benefits beyond its contribution to survival. "Instinctively," she said, "I felt that we all need a little boredom in our lives."

Mann devised an experiment wherein a group of participants was given the most boring assignment she could think of: copying, by hand, phone numbers from the phone book. (For some of you who might never have seen one of those, Google it.) This was based on a classic creativity test developed in 1967 by J. P. Guilford, an American psychologist and one of the first researchers to study creativity. Guilford's original Alternative Uses Test gave subjects two minutes to come up with as many uses as they could think of for everyday objects such as cups, paper clips, or a chair. In Mann's version, she preceded the creativity test with twenty minutes of a meaningless task: in this case, copying numbers out of the phone book. Afterward, her subjects were asked to come up with as many uses as they could for two paper cups (the kind you get at an ecologically unscrupulous water cooler). The participants devised mildly original ideas for their cups, such as plant pots and sand-box toys.

In the next experiment, Mann ratcheted up the boring quotient. Instead of copying numbers out of the phone book for twenty minutes, this time they had to read the phone numbers out loud. Although a handful of people actually enjoyed this task (go figure) and were excused from the study, the vast majority of participants found reading the phone book absolutely, stultifyingly boring. It's more difficult to space out when engaged in an active task such as writing than when doing something as passive as reading. The result, as Mann had hypothesized, was even more creative ideas for the paper cups, including earrings, telephones, all kinds of musical instruments, and, Mann's favorite, a Madonna-style bra. This group thought beyond the cup-as-container.

By means of these experiments, Mann proved her point: People who are bored think more creatively than those who aren't.

But what exactly happens when you get bored that ignites your imagination? "When we're bored, we're searching for something to stimulate us that we can't find in our immediate surroundings," Mann explained. "So we might try to find that stimulation by our minds wandering and going off someplace in our heads. That is what can stimulate creativity, because once you start daydreaming and allow your mind to wander, you start thinking beyond the conscious and into the subconscious. This process allows different connections to take place. It's really awesome." *Totally* awesome.

Boredom is the gateway to mind-wandering, which helps our brains create those new connections that can solve anything from planning dinner to a breakthrough in combating global warming. Researchers have only recently begun to understand the phenomenon of mind-wandering, the activity our brains engage in when we're doing something boring, or doing nothing at all. Most of the studies on the neuroscience of daydreaming have only been done within the past ten years. With modern brain-imaging technology, discoveries are emerging every day about what our brains are doing not only when we are deeply engaged in an activity but also when we space out.

Mind-Wandering or the Default Mode

When we're consciously doing things—even writing down numbers in a phone book—we're using the "executive attention network," the parts of the brain that control and inhibit our attention. As neuroscientist Marcus Raichle put it, "The attention network makes it possible for us to relate directly to the world around us, i.e., here and now." By contrast, when our minds wander, we activate a part of our brain called the "default mode network," which was discovered by Raichle. The default mode, a term also coined by Raichle, is used to describe the brain "at rest"; that is, when we're not focused on an external, goal-oriented task. So, contrary to the popular view, when we space out, our minds aren't switched off.

"Scientifically, daydreaming is an interesting phenomenon because it speaks to the capacity that people have to create thought in a pure way rather than thought happening when it's a response to events in the outside world," said Jonathan Smallwood, who has studied mind-wandering since the beginning of his career in neuroscience, twenty years ago. (Perhaps not coincidentally, the year he finished his PhD was the same year the default mode was discovered.)

Smallwood—who is so enamored with mind-wandering, it's his Twitter handle—explained why his discipline is still in its infancy. "It has an interesting place in the history of psychology and neuroscience simply because of the way cognitive science is organized," he said. "Most experimental paradigms and theories tend to involve us showing something to the brain or the mind and watching what happens." For most of the past, this task-driven method has been used to figure out how the brain functions, and it has produced a tremendous amount of knowledge regarding how we adapt to external stimuli. "Mind-wandering is special because it doesn't fit into that phenomenon," Smallwood said.

We're at a pivotal point in the history of neuroscience, according to Smallwood, because, with the advent of brain imaging and other comprehensive tools for figuring out what's going on in there, we are beginning to understand functioning that has until now escaped study. And that includes what we experience when we're off-task or, no pun intended, in our own heads.

The crucial nature of daydreaming became obvious to Smallwood almost as soon as he began to study it. Spacing out is so important to us as a species that "it could be at the crux of what makes humans different from less complicated animals." It is involved in a wide variety of skills, from creativity to projecting into the future.

There is still so much to discover in the field, but what's definitely clear is that the default mode is not a state where the brain is inactive. Smallwood uses functional magnetic resonance imaging (fMRI) to explore what neural changes occur when test subjects lie in a scanner and do nothing but stare at a fixed image.

It turns out that in the default mode, we're still tapping about 95 percent of the energy we use when our brains are engaged in hard-core, focused thinking. Despite being in an inattentive state, our brains are still doing a remarkable amount of work. While people were lying in scanners in Smallwood's experiment, their brains continued to "exhibit very organized spontaneous activity."

"We don't really understand why it's doing it," he said. "When you're given nothing to do, your thoughts don't stop. You continue to generate thought even when there's nothing for you to do *with* the thoughts."

Part of what Smallwood and his team are working on is trying to connect this state of unconstrained self-generated thought and that of organized, spontaneous brain activity, because they see the two states as "different sides of the same coin."

The areas of the brain that make up the default mode network—the medial temporal lobe, the medial prefrontal cortex, and the posterior cingulate cortex—are turned off when we engage in attention-demanding tasks. But they are very active in autobiographical memory (our personal archive of life experiences); theory of mind (essentially, our ability to imagine what others are thinking and feeling); and—this one's a doozy—self-referential processing (basically, crafting a coherent sense of self).

When we lose focus on the outside world and drift inward, we're not shutting down. We're tapping into a vast trove of memories, imagining future possibilities, dissecting our interactions with other people, and reflecting on who we are. It feels like we are wasting time when we wait for the longest red light in the world to turn green, but the brain is putting ideas and events into perspective.

This gets to the heart of why mind-wandering or daydreaming is different from other forms of cognition. Rather than experiencing, organizing, and understanding things based on how they come to us from the outside world, we do it from within our own cognitive system. That allows for reflection and the ability for greater understanding after the heat of the moment. Smallwood gives the example of an argument: While it's happening, it's hard to be objective or see things from the perspective of the other person. Anger and adrenaline, as well as the physical and emotional presence of another human being, get in the way of contemplation. But in the shower or on a drive the next day, when your brain relives the argument, your thoughts become more nuanced. You not only think of a million things you should have said, but, perhaps, without the "stimulus that is the person you were arguing with," you might get another perspective and gain insights. Thinking in a different way about a personal interaction, rather than the way you did when you encountered it in the real world, is a profound form of creativity spurred on by mind-wandering.

"Daydreaming is especially crucial for a species like ours, where social interactions are important," Smallwood said. "That's because in day-to-day life, the most unpredictable things you encounter are other people." If you break it down, most of our world, from traffic lights to grocery store checkouts, is actually governed by very simple sets of rules. People—not so much. "Daydreaming reflects the need to make sense of complicated aspects of life, which is almost always other human beings."

It's not called the default state for nothing. We may be absorbed in mind-wandering for up to 50 percent of our waking hours. (Think about that. Now—don't.)

The Reality of Daydreams

Daydreams can give us new insight—or they can entertain or energize us. They are as unique as the individual dreaming them up. Still, researchers have found some generalizations. The younger you are, the more you daydream; children and teenagers daydream the most. As we get older, we still daydream about the future, but less about goals or sex—and we have fewer hostile or revenge daydreams. Eric Klinger, professor of psychology at the University of Minnesota, breaks daydreams into the two most common recurring themes: the conquering hero and the suffering martyr. The conquering hero daydream involves success and power—like signing a record contract, hitting the game-winning home run, or overcoming a psychological obstacle such as fear. The suffering martyr's daydreams, on the other hand, are scenes played out in which a person is at first unappreciated but eventually acknowledged for his or her accomplishments or merit. Based on anecdotal evidence, men report having more conquering hero daydreams and women more of the suffering martyr kind.

The Dark Side to Spacing Out

Talking to Professor Smallwood had me more convinced than ever that it's destructive to fill all the cracks in our day with checking e-mail, updating Twitter, or incessantly patting our pockets or bag to check for a vibrating phone. I saw why letting one's mind wander really *is* the key to creativity and productivity.

"Well, that's a contentious statement," Smallwood said. "I mean, people whose minds wander all the time wouldn't get anything done."

Fair point. I didn't like that Smallwood was trying to slow me down, but, true enough, daydreaming hasn't always been considered a good thing. Freud thought daydreamers were neurotic. As late as the 1960s, teachers were warned that daydreaming students were at risk for mental health issues.

There are obviously different ways to daydream or mind-wander—and not all of them are productive or positive. In his seminal book *The Inner World of Daydreaming*, psychologist Jerome L. Singer, who has been studying mind-wandering for more than fifty years, identifies three different styles of daydreaming:

- poor attention control
- guilty-dysphoric
- positive-constructive

And, yes, they are just what they sound like. People with poor attention control are anxious, easily distracted, and have difficulty concentrating, even on their daydreams.

When our mind-wandering is dysphoric, our thoughts drift to unproductive and negative places. We berate ourselves for having forgotten an important birthday or obsess over failing to come up with a clever retort when we needed one. We're flooded with emotions like guilt, anxiety, and anger. For some of us, it's easy to get trapped in this cycle of negative thinking. Not surprisingly, this kind of mind-wandering is more frequent in people who report chronic levels of unhappiness. When dysphoric mind-wandering becomes chronic, it can lead people into destructive behaviors like compulsive gambling, addiction, and eating disorders.

The question, however, is whether mind-wandering is not only more frequent in people who report chronic levels of unhappiness, but whether it also *promotes* unhappiness. In a 2010 study called "A Wandering Mind Is an Unhappy Mind" (gulp), Harvard psychologists Matthew Killingsworth and Daniel Gilbert developed an iPhone app to survey the thoughts, feelings, and actions of five thousand people at any given time throughout a day. (When a chime went off randomly on the participant's smartphone, up popped a series of questions that touched on what the person was doing, if he was thinking about what he was doing, and how happy he was, among other things.) From the results of the survey, Killingsworth and Gilbert found that "people are thinking about what is not happening almost as often as they are thinking about what is" and "doing so typically makes them unhappy."

It's just like what you hear in every yoga class—the key to happiness is being in the moment. So what's the deal? Is mind-wandering productive or self-defeating? Well, it seems that, like everything else in life, day-dreaming is complicated.

Smallwood coauthored a study on the relationship between mood and mind-wandering that found "the generation of thoughts unrelated to the current environment may be both a cause and a consequence of un-happiness." *What!?*

The 2013 study (coauthored by Florence J. M. Ruby, Haakon En-gen, and Tania Singer) argues that not all kinds of self-generated thought or mind-wandering are alike. The data collected from ap-proximately one hundred participants took into account whether their thoughts were task related, focused on the past or future, about them-selves or others, and positive or negative. What this study found was that, yes, negative thoughts brought about negative moods (no duh). Self-generated thought in depressed people tended to cause and be caused by negative moods, and "past-related thought may be especially likely to be associated with low mood." But all hope is not lost. The study also found that "by contrast, future- and self-related thoughts pre-ceded improvements of mood, even when current thought content was negative."

"Daydreaming has aspects that will allow us to think originally about our lives," Smallwood told me. "But in certain circumstances, continu-ing to think about something might not be the right thing to do. Many states of chronic unhappiness are probably linked to daydreaming sim-ply because there are unsolvable problems."

Mind-wandering is not unlike our smartphones, where you can easily have too much of a good thing. Smallwood argues that we shouldn't think about the technology of our phones—or our brains—in terms of the value judgments "good" or "bad." Rather it comes down to how we put them to use. "Smartphones allow us to do all kinds of amazing things like contact people from great distances, but we can get trapped in de-voting our entire life to them," he said. "That's not the smartphone's fault." Daydreaming gets us to think about things in a different way, for good, bad, or, well, just different.

MIND-BENDING FACTS ABOUT MIND-WANDERING
- When some people daydream, they think about the future and often long-term goals. "Prospective bias," as this is called, has been documented in Europe, the United States, China, and Japan.
- People whose minds wander into the future are more likely to delay gratification and have higher levels of attention control.
- Mind-wandering has its time and place, though. It unfortunately has been associated with automobile accidents. (Smallwood's tip: "Try to limit the amount of daydreaming you do when you're operating heavy machinery.")

The flip side of dysphoric daydreaming, the positive-constructive kind, is when our thoughts veer toward the imaginative. We get excited about the possibilities that our brain can conjure up seemingly out of nowhere, like magic. This mode of mind-wandering reflects our internal drive to explore ideas and feelings, make plans, and problem-solve.

So how can we engage in healthy mind-wandering? Let's say you had a tiff with your coworker. That night, while making a salad, you find yourself replaying the scene over and over in your mind; waves of anger wash over you yet again as you berate yourself for not having come up with a wittier retort to his underhanded comment implying you hadn't pulled your weight during a recent project. But with positive-constructive mind-wandering, you'd get over the past and come up with a way to show him all the legwork these projects require of you . . . or maybe you resolve to be put on another team altogether and avoid the jerk entirely because life's too short.

"It's easier said than done to change your thinking," Smallwood said. "Daydreaming is different from many other forms of distraction in that when your thoughts wander to topics, they're telling you something about where your life is and how you feel about where it is. The problem with that is sometimes when people's lives aren't going so well, daydreaming might feel more difficult than it would be at times when their lives are going great. Either way, the point is that it does provide insight into who we are."

All those hours I spent as a new mother, pushing my colicky baby in a stroller because he wouldn't sleep any other way and wishing I could be more productive or in touch with what was going on in the rest of society, were actually incredibly useful, because I had unwittingly been letting my mind have space and time to travel much further than ever before. I not only tapped into past experiences but also imagined myself in future places of my own design, doing autobiographical planning. While ruminating on painful experiences or dwelling on the past is definitely a very real by-product of daydreaming, research by Small- wood and others has shown that, when given time for self-reflection, most people tend toward "prospective bias." That kind of thinking helps us come up with new solutions—like, in my case, a whole new career. By design, daydreaming is helpful to us when we're stuck on a problem, personal, professional, or otherwise. And boredom is one of the best catalysts to kick-start the process.

Boredom and Brilliance

At first glance, boredom and brilliance are completely at odds with each other. Boredom, if defined just as the state of being weary and restless through lack of interest, overwhelmingly has negative connotations and should be avoided at all costs, whereas brilliance is something we aspire to—a quality of striking success and unusual mental ability. Genius, in- tellect, talent, flair versus languidness, dullness, doldrums. It's not im- mediately apparent, but these two opposing states are in fact intimately connected.

Andreas Elpidorou, a researcher in the Department of Philosophy at the University of Louisville and self-described defender of boredom, ex- plains, "Boredom motivates the pursuit of a new goal when the current goal ceases to be satisfactory, attractive, or meaningful [to you]." In his 2014 academic article "The Bright Side of Boredom," Elpidorou argues that boredom "acts as a regulatory state that keeps one in line with one's projects. In the absence of boredom, one would remain trapped in unfulfilling situations and miss out on many emotionally, cognitively, and socially rewarding experiences. Boredom is both a warning that we are not doing what we want to be doing and a 'push' that motivates us to switch goals and projects."

You could say that boredom is an incubator lab for brilliance. It's the messy, uncomfortable, confusing, frustrating place one has to occupy for a while before finally coming up with the winning equation or formula. This narrative has been repeated many, many times. *The Hobbit* was conceived when J.R.R. Tolkien, a professor at Oxford, "got an enormous pile of exam papers there and was marking school examinations in the summer time, which was very laborious, and unfortunately also boring." When he came upon one exam page a student had left blank, he was overjoyed. "Glorious! Nothing to read," Tolkien told the BBC in 1968. "So I scribbled on it, I can't think why, 'In a hole in the ground there lived a hobbit.'" And so, the opening line of one of the most beloved works of fantasy fiction was born. Steve Jobs, who changed the world with his popular vision of technology, famously said, "I'm a big believer in boredom. . . . All the [technology] stuff is wonderful, but having nothing to do can be wonderful, too." In a *Wired* piece by Steven Levy, the cofounder of Apple—nostalgic for the long, boring summers of his youth that stoked his curiosity because "out of curiosity comes everything"—expressed concern about the erosion of boredom from the kind of devices he helped create.

When it came to brilliance, Steve Jobs was the master. So let's take him up on his advice to embrace boredom. Let your knowledge of the science and history behind boredom inspire you to bring it back into your life. You might feel uncomfortable, annoyed, or even angry at first, but who knows what you can accomplish once you get through the first phases of boredom and start triggering some of its amazing side effects?

What Is Boredom?

Boredom is necessary

We need to reclaim this word. Boredom has been hijacked and equated with mediocrity. "Only boring people get bored," parents love to say. But clearly that's not the case. When you're bored, you are, in reality, opening the gateway to feeding, nurturing, and cultivating your thoughts. Your mind needs boredom to do some of its most important work.

Boredom is a state of mind

In scientific terms, when you get bored, you activate a neural network in the brain called the default mode. Some scientists even refer to it as the imagination network, because our most original ideas can take shape there. Throughout the ages, artists, builders, and thinkers of all kinds have engaged in what Jerome Singer calls "positive-constructive daydreaming" in order to tap into new ways to look at the world around them.

Boredom is productive

We think of being bored as a waste of time, and yet boredom can spark goal-setting, strategizing, and essential autobiographical planning. So while it may not feel productive at first, boredom helps us find meaning at every level of existence.

Boredom is a wake-up call

Sherry Turkle put it best when she said, "Boredom is telling you that this is a moment for your imagination, for your creativity, for your identity. Boredom is telling you to pay attention to the world." It's telling you it's time to put down the cell phone and lift up your head to the great wide world around you!

What Is Brilliance?

Brilliance is humble

Brilliance doesn't have to look like Nobel Prize–winning work on quantum electrodynamics or a painting from the Renaissance. It can be finding a way to help your child make friends at school or pinning down what aspect of your job makes you happy. Though brilliance may be small and simple, that doesn't make it any less powerful.

Brilliance is subversive

Anyone who puts together a complex Lego kit needs smarts. But building an intricate, one-of-a-kind structure with thousands of Lego pieces requires unconventional thinking. Brilliance has a twinkle to it. It's spirited, and sometimes even a little bit naughty. You may need to keep those brilliant flashes of insight and inspiration to yourself because they may not always be socially appropriate. As one of my favorite writers, Walter Kirn, explained to me, "If you have nothing to hide, then you have nothing going on." Without an interior life in which to blossom, thoughts are flat, unremarkable. Not brilliant in the slightest.

Brilliance is predictable

Ideas seem to spark when we least expect it, such as while walking the dog or brushing our teeth. That's the default mode at work; when our body is at rest, or doing a menial task, our mind is at its busiest. By building our capacity for boredom, instead of trying to escape it, we can give brilliance an opportunity to flash more often (with the added perk of getting the laundry done).

Brilliance is slow

Combining disparate ideas into a wholly new entity takes time, solitude, and a tolerance for tedium. And yet we rarely give ourselves these conditions at work, at home, or even in our own minds. By rushing to get things done and accomplish more tasks (sometimes simultaneously) we actually come up with fewer novel solutions that have real lasting impact.

Brilliance is sometimes very mundane

Doing something better, faster, or more safely is definitely brilliant. Surgical teams in eight hospitals adopted a simple pre-procedure checklist and reduced death rates by 40 percent. On the home front, loading each type of silverware into its own compartment in the dishwasher makes unloading faster and life a little easier. Originality counts, but sometimes a small tweak makes a big difference.

2

Digital Overload

*It didn't make me feel good. It made me feel
bad instead. So I stopped.*

—Louis C.K. on why he quit Twitter

One of the first things I did in my quest to explore boredom was spend a morning sitting on a Manhattan street corner. People-watching in New York City is never boring, but I wanted to tally how many people were making absolutely sure they had no possibility of getting bored. In other words, how many folks couldn't walk down the street in the greatest city in the world without the help of some sort of gadget?

In my very unscientific study, out of the 1,000 people who passed me, I counted 315 of them typing on, looking at, listening to, or just gripping their phone. (Just having your phone at the ready can make you less engaged with your surroundings. There's no way it can be completely out of your mind if you still have your phone in sight. Also, have you ever managed *not* to look at an object that starts buzzing in your hand?) My small sampling showed a third of all pedestrians that day were using their phones in some way. A more official study done by the City University of New York's Lehman College in 2015 found that nearly *half* the pedestrians at five busy Manhattan intersections were so distracted by their electronic devices that they ignored red lights when crossing the street. "Wexting" (walking while texting) can be dangerous, but when even the Big Apple (or the threat of being run over) can't compete for our attention, you know this must be love.

Those little phones have such a powerful hold over us that some people find them nearly impossible to put down. Thanks to mobile phones, we're now privy to a limitless array of seductive, easily accessed, and often free entertainment, ways to connect, and a million other tools to make us better and faster at everything we do. It's not too much to say that our devices have transformed almost every minute of our day. And while technology has made possible so much that was unthinkable only ten years ago, there are unintended consequences, both positive and negative.

I have a whip-smart colleague who always has the best ideas for shows and edits—but who also can't keep from checking Instagram while our audio engineer makes a change. Even when we play back the sound edit, she can't help herself. "J, what did you think?" I'll ask. "Did that work for you?"

"Argh, sorry! Can you play it again?" she asks, trying desperately to tear herself away.

We all have personal examples of work meetings grown flabby and unfocused, lunches with friends that take place half in the present, and half with other online friends. Time gets nibbled away. That's not to say that keeping up with friends on Instagram isn't fun or even important. But doing those kinds of things can be detrimental to what is happening in your life *right now*. Why not enjoy or increase productivity in virtual and physical reality by not occupying both realms simultaneously? When neither activity is given time to blossom into a true experience, it's like one long mental snack. At the end of the day, you aren't even full and you just feel bloated.

I'm far from the only one who finds technology intrusive. When we did the Bored and Brilliant challenge, so many *Note to Self* listeners described their issues of digital self-control—like Eric, a high school teacher with a Twitter problem. "I use my phone in the classroom as a timer and to look things up that my students are wondering about (they are always wondering about something)," he said. "But I also find myself wanting to tweet while I'm there, and that doesn't exactly inspire confidence in me."

As a new teacher, Eric was simultaneously energized by the many new experiences and ideas surrounding him all day long. While technology worked for him as an easy and convenient tool in the classroom, he also struggled with the lure of its limitlessness. Unable to keep himself from accessing things at the wrong place and time, he wound up feeling amped up and distracted. But when he tried to channel all that youthful enthusiasm into something more productive: "In the evenings when I come home, I want to write, I want to think," he said, "and I just can't and I get sucked into my phone." Eric hoped that Bored and Brilliant would be a way to "jump-start" his brain.

Notes on Digital Overload

Here are some thoughts and reflections from real people who did the Bored and Brilliant challenge:

"Mobile technology was sold as the ability to connect with anyone, at any time. It has delivered tenfold on that promise, and we are now constantly entranced by innumerable digital baubles that lure us into endless swiping and tapping for hours on end. I believe my phone should be able to augment my experience of the world around me, not become the world around me. Too many ideas are subverted by freemium distraction. It is time to recalibrate this relationship and achieve a new, more productive symbiosis."

—Barbara

"I have been feeling too drawn to my iPad recently, and it's all for relatively meaningless stuff. I keep being reminded that life is short and I know I will be full of regrets about the role the iPad played in my life when I'm running out of days. :/"

—Sophia

"I'd like to be able to sit and read and not interrupt myself every five minutes to check *Clash of Clans*; or to watch an hour-long drama and really appreciate all the nuances which I've been missing because I'm only spending 30 percent of my attention on it."

—Liam

What's making this all happen? "The world is more addictive than it was forty years ago," wrote Paul Graham, the famous programmer, investor, and thinker on technology. The founder of Y Combinator (a tech incubator that's funded over a thousand start-ups, including Dropbox, Airbnb, and Reddit), is not alone in his assessment. Golden Krishna, an expert in user experience who currently works on design strategy at Google, astutely pointed out during one of our conversations that the only people who refer to their customers as "users" are drug dealers—and technologists.

Many of us who have observed our own behavior don't need science to prove that technology is altering us, but let's bring some in anyway. Dopamine, the neurotransmitter that records certain experiences in our brain (typically described as pleasurable) and prompts us to repeat them, plays a part not only in sex and drugs, but also the swiping and tapping that we do on our smartphones.

Scott Barry Kaufman—scientific director of the Imagination Institute, a nonprofit dedicated to advocating for imagination "across all sectors of society"—gave me the straight dope on dopamine. "It's a misconception that dopamine has to do with our feelings of happiness or pleasure," he said. "It's a molecule that helps influence our expectations." Higher levels of dopamine are linked to being more open to new things and novelty seeking. Something novel could be an amazing idea for dinner or a new book . . . or just getting likes on a Facebook post or the ping of a text coming in. Our digital devices activate and hijack this dopamine system extremely well, when we let them.

"Research shows that great artists, scientists, and other types of creators have an abundance of dopamine in their system that allows them to deal with novelty," Kaufman explained. In other words, they are extra-motivated to seek out the new and can then channel that novelty seeking into being creative. Kaufman calls dopamine "the mother of invention" and explains that because we have a limited amount of it, we must be judicious about choosing to spend it on "increasing our wonder and excitement for creating meaning and new things like art—or on Twitter."

Well, when you put it like that, I almost want to deactivate my Twitter account. *Almost.*

A constant flow of incoming information is something many of us have come to expect, even need. Dr. Mary Helen Immordino-Yang says this kind of technology use is how "habits," in exactly the behavioral scientific sense of the word, develop.

"It's a content-, context-specific reflex that we teach ourselves to do by habitual practice," she said. And, as with many habits, once developed, it's a struggle to turn off, even if we want to. All it takes is one little ping from the phone to interrupt a potentially creative, productive, and internally focused state of mind, whether we are absorbed in a craft project, listening to beautiful music, or astounded by an incredible mountain view. "We're like lab rats conditioned to check our phones way more often than we need to in order to be responsible workers or friends," Immordino-Yang said.

We've trained our brains to always have one thumb on Snapchat. But if we want to, we can also untrain them. "We have to mindfully step back and say, wait a minute, I don't need any more information to make sense out of whatever I'm doing," Immordino-Yang said. "Let me stop and reflect." She admits, however, that her prescription is tough to do. Stepping back or, rather, logging off is difficult because of the "insidious way this kind of technology takes over your mental space."

"It's not supported for us societally to withdraw to take time for yourself," said Immordino-Yang. But she thinks we are at a pivotal moment as more and more people are beginning to realize they need to take an active role in monitoring their digital life. Right now, thanks to business models built on hours spent with your eyeballs, technologists would prefer you never look away from a screen again. In light of that, self-regulation is a backlash to products co-opting our attention spans. That's certainly what I heard from the thousands of *Note to Self* listeners who embarked on the Bored and Brilliant challenge. They not only felt like they wanted to reclaim the space to *think* instead of bulldozing over it with various forms of entertainment, but they also wanted to do it *as soon as possible*. The imperative comes from the fact that the longer we mindlessly use our devices, the more control they have over us. The effects are cumulative.

Not everyone believes that the Information Age will have real implications for how our brains will work and adapt to the tech world around us. Although all this technology is so new, any ideas about its long-standing effects are still just theories; there's a schism forming between those who think digital addiction is a "thing" and on its way to becoming a big societal problem and those who say these warnings are just the latest in a long line of fear over any kind of technological advance.

A 2015 Pew Research Center study on the relationship between stress and technology investigated the claims from critics that "these technologies take over people's lives, creating time pressures that put people at risk for the negative physical and psychological health effects that can result from stress." A survey of 1,801 participants about whether their use of social media, cell phones, and the Internet was associated with higher levels of stress found that "overall, frequent Internet and social media users *do not* have higher levels of stress." The study found a connection between technology and stress only when "there are circumstances under which the social use of digital technology increases awareness of stressful events in the lives of others." So any negative impact of digital use doesn't have to do with frequency or volume but rather the nature of the content—no different from the terrible feeling you might have after watching the local TV news.

One of the study's authors, Keith Hampton—a professor at Rutgers School of Communication and Information whose research focuses on the relationship between new information and communication technologies, social networks, democratic engagement, and the urban environment—says the data proves our concerns over social media, gadgets, and games are just the same as when previous generations fretted over the introduction of the radio, television, or cars.

"We've had moral panics about new technologies for centuries," Hampton said. "Muslim scholars in the fourteenth century were talking about info overload, too many books. A hundred years ago we were concerned about this new phenomenon of dads sitting at kitchen tables reading newspapers instead of spending time with their wives and children. I don't think much has changed. A new technology, a new moral panic."

Tell that to Cynan Clucas, a British father of four and digital marketing exec who blames his adult-onset ADHD on the very technology he uses all the time to make him smarter.

Is Technology Giving Us ADHD?
The Case of Cynan Clucas

Cynan's problems with his brain began three years ago—or at least that's when he started to notice a significant decline in his ability to manage tasks. "There were gaps in my performance, gaps in my memory, gaps in my ability to adjust my routine on a day-to-day basis to cope with whatever was coming," he said. Those weren't the only outward signs of trouble inside his head.

The company Cynan started fourteen years ago has an open-plan office, and he used to take pride in keeping his desk as neat as a pin, with everything lined up just so. Now it's become a metaphor for Cynan's muddled mind. "I can't even describe how disorganized it is," he said. "It's just piles of paper around a twenty-seven-inch iMac with a keyboard and several cups. Honestly, it's more than a metaphor, it's a mirror of my mental experience."

Last year, when a few key employees left the company in quick succession (for reasons like relocation and career progression), their departure highlighted how they had picked up the slack around him and managed the chaos he created. The people Cynan hired to replace them couldn't support him in the same way, so projects became disorganized, clients grew unhappy, and his staff became increasingly frustrated. Panicked that his chaotic mental state was beginning to affect his company, Cynan went to see his doctor. Although he was only in his early forties, Cynan worried he might be suffering from early-onset dementia. He had read about people his age with similar symptoms to his receiving that diagnosis.

His doctor ran a battery of tests—Alzheimer's, blood, thyroid—but they all came back negative. The diagnosis his doctor finally returned with truly shocked Cynan: "You present the most profound symptoms of any adult that I've seen to support an ADHD diagnosis."

Attention deficit hyperactivity disorder? To Cynan's mind, that was something only children got—and American children, at that. In England, doctors don't hand out ADHD diagnoses as frequently as they do here (only 1.5 percent of British children are diagnosed with the disorder, as compared to 6 percent of American kids), leading many Brits to question whether it's even a real thing. Firmly in this skeptical camp, Cynan didn't think ADHD was real but "something that perhaps the pharmaceutical companies engineered."

If he looked back on his childhood, Cynan always had a lot of independent ideas, projects, and plans going that kept him busy and on the move. Perhaps that could be interpreted as evidence of a distracted mind, but his nature never affected his grades in school or, later, his business . . . at least not until the last three years or so. So what changed?

After reflecting on the differences in his life since his problem with distraction began, he homed in on the major one: technology. Much of Cynan's work is keeping abreast of the latest devices, apps, and online platforms—and then teaching his clients how to use them to attract customers. "It's very important that as a business, we are very focused on learning and adapting to all the new creative tech that comes along," he said.

The more he thought about it, however, the more Cynan realized that as he used these new forms of technology, he was also abdicating his mental responsibilities to them. Basically he had slowly outsourced his brain to apps, online calendars, tracking systems, and social media—and by outsourcing all the work his brain used to do, well, his brain just got used to not working. The irony that using apps to store and manage all his mundane information (like remembering telephone numbers and managing passwords) was supposed to give him more time and space to problem-solve and do high-level thinking, not *less*, is not lost on Cynan. "By delegating to technology, we think that technology somehow is going to resolve problems for us," he said. "But it doesn't, because the more that you delegate, the less your brain has to be engaged."

Cynan's doctors told him that there is no such thing as adult-onset ADHD and that he must have had it throughout his childhood. There's also no proof that his ADHD is a direct result of his digital gadgets. Much of this technology hasn't been around long enough for there to be conclusive studies on how it affects our brains—and it's hard to find a control group of people who aren't on the Internet to compare to the rest of us who wouldn't know how to change a lightbulb (and what voltage and if it's good for the environment and if it's worth investing in a "smart" bulb, etc.) if it weren't for Google. So just to be clear, there's no scientific evidence that tech or the Internet could cause someone to develop the actual disorder of ADHD. But tech moves and changes so fast that we can't always wait around for that peer-reviewed double-blind medical study before we start asking behavioral questions for ourselves.

According to Michael Pietrus, clinical director at the School of the Art Institute of Chicago and an ADHD evaluation expert, all this stuff is indeed affecting our working memory and ability to process information. "Technology and social media can impair those areas, which can either look very similar to ADHD or exacerbate underlying attention problems that people might already have," said Pietrus, who put the current number of those diagnosed with ADHD at around 11 percent of the population. For the college population, that number could be as high as 18 to 20 percent of students who meet the criteria for an ADHD diagnosis. The number of diagnoses of ADHD has gone up tremendously (about 3 to 5 percent every year) in children, adolescents, and young adults over the past ten years. "It's becoming one of the largest-growing minority populations on college campuses," Pietrus said.

Pietrus explained that ADHD is a "rule-out diagnosis," or a "diagnosis of exclusion," meaning that in assessing someone for the disorder, you first try to eliminate all other causes for trouble focusing, such as lack of sleep, substance abuse, anxiety, depression—or too much time on Facebook. "Recently, when I'm doing evaluations with college-age students, I ask them, 'How much time do you spend on the Internet?'" he said. "And more often than not, they give me a look that says, 'I don't even know how to compute that. It's, like, when am I not on the Internet?'"

Of course, students struggled with procrastination, prioritizing, organization, and other issues of time management way before the Internet was invented. That's just a typical phase young adults go through. But digital media presents a particular challenge to those with a tendency toward distraction.

"Folks will get on Facebook for what feels to them like five, ten minutes. Then they look up, and it's been two hours," Pietrus said. "The rapid, repetitive, and intense interactions that can take place on sites like that disconnect us from our sense of time and place."

The psychologist went on to explain that the area of the brain affected by the social media time-suck is the prefrontal cortex, where executive functioning primarily takes place. "Executive functioning is like the orchestra conductor of the brain," he said. "When we're being rewarded consistently, whether it's reading a story or having a picture liked or, you know, playing some kind of video game or something like that, it really impacts our ability to use our executive functioning effectively, and to manage what's going on in our experience."

It's important to get to the root cause if someone is struggling to focus, because the intervention will change depending on whether the issue is a lack of sleep, poor nutrition, overuse of technology, some other mental health concern, or true ADHD (the last of which is treated with a stimulant medication). Rather than tell the college students he works with, "Here, take this pill that's going to help you pay attention in the moment," Pietrus believes framing his patients' issues within a larger context is more beneficial than treating only their symptoms. "Clinically, I talk about intentionality. Being aware of what it is they're doing with their time and their behaviors, being more mindful about the consequence of what they're doing online and off."

And here's the twist with Mike Pietrus—his firsthand knowledge of the effects of technology via his students is supplemented by a deeper knowledge of how the digital media they consume actually works. Pietrus is intimately aware of technology's power to distract because he's married to a social strategist. That's right, his wife's job is to advise advertising clients on the best way to use social and digital media to reach their consumers. It's like the start of a bad joke. Or perhaps just the most complementary coupling ever? Lizz Pietrus is in digital marketing and the business of grabbing your attention, "an increasingly more difficult job," she admits, "when you look at the crush of information that comes through on social platforms every day." The way this crush of information gets delivered is in constant flux, but a major turning point came with the infamous Oreo tweet during Super Bowl XLVII in 2013. A power outage at the arena caused some of the lights to go out for more than a half hour, so the Oreo social media team of fifteen people delivered an ad designed to cash in on the audience's immediate and shared experience: the image of a lone Oreo with the caption, "Power out? No problem. You can still dunk in the dark." Fifteen thousand retweets and twenty thousand likes on Facebook caused the Tumblr account Digg to declare, "Oreo won the Super Bowl blackout."

"It launched this idea of real-time marketing where it was enough for brands to create some funny content that was relevant in the moment," Lizz said. Oreo's social media methodology became copied and codified almost instantaneously. "So brands were just putting tons and tons and tons of content out there in the world, mostly on social platforms. What we failed to recognize was whether or not that did anything from a business standpoint." Do we really buy and eat more Oreos? Maybe we just pay more attention to the clever and ever-changing ways we get served stimulation. Lizz now advises her clients to be thoughtful about the content they put on social media. "It's getting harder and harder for our short-term memory, which is already limited, to retain information, because there's just so much information coming at us by people like me."

According to her husband, Mike, though, Lizz is in the minority. He sees few brands or digital platforms showing restraint. Instead, they are honing their tactics and getting "very effective at pulling people into these behavioral loops."

"Internet use can be like drugs and gambling and shopping and pornography all wrapped up into one," Mike said. "And while it isn't in the *DSM-5* just yet, it's clear that Internet use and arousal addiction are compelling problems . . . that we have to be able to contain more effectively."

Mike includes himself in the category of those sucked in by other smart, talented people whose jobs are to work night and day, creating ever-new and seductive forms of technology that bank on our attention. Even he admits to having ten to twenty tabs open on his browser, because "there are so many things I feel like I need to read, watch, or listen to." In fact, in a personal effort to strike back at all the distractions, a couple of weeks before our conversation, Mike deactivated his Facebook account . . . for a while.

"It's up to us to figure out how and where we want to share our attention," he said. "Through research on neuroplasticity, we know that the brain is responsive in that it changes based on the behaviors we adopt, and knowing that is power."

People feel unable to focus and yet companies need to grab consumers' attention to drive the wheels of capitalism. This tension is at the heart of the conflict so many feel right now. Cynan Clucas, the digital marketing exec from earlier, epitomizes and personifies this conflict most dramatically. His mind is shot, he's been diagnosed with ADHD, and yet Cynan's business and very livelihood are built on helping companies use tech in just the way he believes has mentally hurt him. "It's vexing," he said. "I still need to do work to support my family and pay the salaries of the people who work for me so they can pay their mortgages. I don't have the luxury to start a new movement for responsible creative technology or pivoting into a digital creative agency into that space that says, let's slow down. But if there were a demand for it, I would willingly jump in that direction."

The Shocking Things We Do to Avoid Boredom

A team of researchers, led by University of Virginia psychologist Tim Wilson and Harvard's Dan Gilbert, conducted a series of experiments on fifty-five undergrads to find out just how uncomfortable people are when they're doing nothing.

In the beginning, each college student went alone into a windowless, "unadorned" room with simple furniture to minimize any visual stimulation. Once inside the room, they were exposed to different stimuli, like music and pictures, and given mild electric shocks. The researchers then asked if they would pay to avoid being shocked again. Not surprisingly, most of them—forty-two out of fifty-five, in fact—said they would pay to avoid a jolt.

Here's where things get interesting. After this conversation, each student was told to spend the next fifteen minutes alone "just thinking"—but they could press a button to give themselves a shock if they wanted to.

Did they do it? You bet. And, yes, even people who had said they would pay money to avoid getting shocked again pressed that button. The results from Wilson and Gilbert's experiment, published in the July 2014 issue of *Science*, revealed that one-third of the men and a quarter of the women were so unnerved by the boredom, they preferred to take any available form of distraction—even if it meant a shock. One participant shocked himself 190 times!

Reading Incomprehension

"As people in creative technology, we talk about the value of disruption. How disruption is the great innovator and disruption is what gets you scale and funding—all of these phrases that we hear at conferences over and over," Cynan said. "The bottom line for me is that disruption has significantly altered the neuroplasticity of my brain. It's changed how my brain works. I can no longer sit and read a printed page, because my brain can't concentrate long enough to be able to remember the paragraph at the top of the page by the time it reaches the bottom."

We are being affected by our consumption of information on these new digital platforms in so many different ways—from wasting time to trouble sleeping. But many of my *Note to Self* listeners also deeply related to how the Internet is riding roughshod over another technological innovation, albeit one that's considerably older: the printed page.

Along the lines of Cynan's lament, dozens of people wrote me to say that they can no longer get through a novel or even a magazine article. One listener, Katherine, complained that she can't "sit and read for more than fifteen minutes at a time without feeling the urge to jump up and look at my phone."

This very same issue plagued the *Washington Post* writer Mike Rosenwald, a man who gets paid to read, think, and write.

Mike recalled with horror how one night he was reading a new Lorrie Moore short story collection only to find his eyes skipping around the page, much like scrolling on Twitter or Facebook. He couldn't focus. The words weren't coming fast enough. Mike started skimming despite wanting to read and immerse himself in the text. "It occurred to me I was starting to do this a lot," he said. Putting on his reporter hat, Mike called some friends to do an informal poll on whether or not they, too, were having a harder time paying attention while reading. "They were like, 'Oh my God, this is totally my life,'" Mike said.

His journalistic interest piqued, Mike began investigating why he and his friends were struggling with something that, until recently, had come naturally. He went, of course, straight to the Internet to see what was coming between him and the page. (When in Rome . . .) What he discovered was a radical break in reading methodology post-Internet. Before the Web, reading was primarily a linear activity. "You looked at a magazine, a menu, a book. Whatever," he said. "You pretty much read it uninterrupted, and that's the way we've read since writing on caves."

Then along came the Internet with hyperlinks, scrolling screens, and an impossible-to-finish flow of information, which necessitated nonlinear reading. The problem, Mike found, wasn't that our brains have adapted to this second form of reading. Rather, it has supplanted the first. In an article he wrote for *The Washington Post*, he did his own in-house (and meta) experiment on the thoroughness of reading online. Only 30 percent of the people reading his story about having trouble reading got to the last line of his story.

"I was stunned and deeply disturbed," Mike said. "There are things in our lives, whether they be novels, short stories, mortgage documents, that actually need our slow reading. . . . But all the researchers I talk to say you can't put the genie back in the bottle."

Slow reading, cracking open a book, stopping and thinking about a sentence, maybe going back and reading it again. Giving each word a chance to wow or impress or educate you. Is it possible to be a deep and thoughtful reader—and an efficient online skimmer? Can't we do both? This feeling that there's a battle going on between those two skills in our brains comes as no surprise to Maryanne Wolf, director of the Center for Reading and Language Research at Tufts University. Her groundbreaking book, *Proust and the Squid: The Story and Science of the Reading Brain*, was published nearly a decade ago. Thanks to screens, reading has changed a lot since then. So when I reached Maryanne, she was hard at work on an update (*Letters to the Good Reader: The Future of the Reading Brain in a Digital World*), perched next to a small lake in the embrace of the French Alps with very spotty Wi-Fi. The perfect place to concentrate.

The cognitive neuroscientist has an explanation for what was happening to Mike and the rest of us—and the written word: "Our research is beginning to show us that there are various aspects of the reading brain circuit that are changing along with the amount of time that we are spending on the Internet and digital reading."

One study by Anne Mangen of Norway's University of Stavanger looked at the metrics of comprehension when people read on-screen versus on paper. In this experiment, fifty adults read a mystery short story, with half reading the paperback version, and the other half on a Kindle e-reader. Afterward, readers filled out a questionnaire. All reacted in emotionally similar ways to the story, but there was a big difference in how they answered questions about plot chronology. The Kindle readers performed significantly worse when asked to place fourteen events that happened in the story in the correct order. Most of the subjects also showed an "overwhelming preference for print."

Despite the benefits of reading the old-fashioned way, as evidenced in Mangen's study and many others like it, according to Wolf, the human brain is adapting almost too well to the particular attributes or characteristics of Internet reading. Basically, we are losing our ability to slow-read by giving up the practice of it. "That's my real worry," Wolf said. "I worry we will not use our most preciously acquired deep-reading processes because we're just given too much stimulation."

Wolf did one amazing experiment on herself but said, "It was a rather disquieting and actually emotional experience for me." She reread one of her most beloved and challenging books, *The Glass Bead Game*, Hermann Hesse's final novel, set in a distant utopian future where all knowledge, from music and art to science and mathematics, has been encapsulated in a complicated game.

"I couldn't do it anymore!" Wolf said of reading her old favorite. "I couldn't slow my reading down to really allocate sufficient attention to what is basically a very difficult and demanding book!" She may be a neuroscientist, but Wolf's brain had changed as well. She decided to begin a regimen of slow reading to rebuild her similarly atrophied muscle. Every day, for two weeks, she forced herself to read and reread *The Glass Bead Game* until she had built back up her tolerance for deep, difficult reading. As Wolf put it, "I had to learn how to read again."

A relief for Wolf and all adults, but what about young adults and children, who don't have the primary deep-reading foundation established by growing up in the pre-Internet age—the generations that have no place of deep, slow reading to return to and rebuild?

"You're putting your finger on my most worrisome concern," Wolf said. "My real worry is on formation of the young's deep-reading processes. That takes time—it takes actually years to form the ability to put inference and background knowledge and analogy and epiphany all together in a child's brain."

Ideally, future generations will be able to cultivate the ability to read slowly and fast—something Wolf calls a biliterate brain: simultaneously building and maintaining the two different ways the brain can read.

"That's going to take some wisdom on our part," said Wolf, who wants to "preserve" traditional ways of reading while incorporating newer ones in a smart and thoughtful way. "It's going to take people like you and me saying pause—pause, society—think about what you are doing, you as adults and you as teachers of the next generation."

In other words, despite the cost of printing and storing them, books should never be completely replaced by digital text. Resources permitting, every reader should strive for a mix of both paper and e-books. Start with paper, build that deep comprehension, and then transition to digital reading, while maintaining the ability to read difficult and longer texts—this is the next step in literacy. The ratio of paper reading to digital will naturally shift as kids grow up and no longer have time for English Lit 101 and *Madame Bovary*, but deep reading is a skill and a muscle that must continuously be exercised. As Wolf wrote in *Proust and the Squid*, "Taking advantage, then, of the wealth of information that is always just a click away demands the use of executive, organizational, critical, and self-monitoring skills to navigate and make sense of the information."

Perhaps students already intuitively understand the importance of print. Naomi Baron, a linguistics professor and researcher at American University, found that 92 percent of university students from within the United States, Slovakia, Japan, and Germany preferred paper books to e-books. Sure, e-books are cheaper, some of the students surveyed allowed, but they also mentioned loving the smell of a paper book and the sense of accomplishment they felt when they flipped the final page.

Because of this interview—and because he loves curling up with paperbacks—I decided not to give my son, Kai, e-books, even though he got a log-in for an online summer reading list from the school librarian. Screens will inevitably come later, so why not focus on developing his ability to deep read first?

Taking Notes by Hand Is Better for Information Retention

I have long suspected what researchers at Princeton and UCLA have proved: that the tactile experience of writing adds an important dimension to the learning process.

That's why Laura Norén—an adjunct professor at the Stern School of Business at New York University—does *not* allow laptops in her classroom. "It's not just about writing down verbatim," said Norén, which is what students do when they type on a computer as opposed to jotting down ideas in longhand, where "they actually have to do some filtering in the process of taking notes. That's what I want them to learn."

Her policy has benefits that go beyond the act of notetaking. "Over the course of the semester, their ability to participate in discussions in class goes up dramatically," Norén said of her students. "At first they're very quiet. They don't know how to interact with each other and only talk to me. As the course goes on, they communicate better with each other, which would not happen if laptops were open."

CHALLENGE ONE: Observe Yourself

The very first challenge in the Bored and Brilliant program is simply to take a good hard look at your true digital usage. Noticing and understanding your baseline behavior from the moment you wake until you go to sleep is the first step in taking control of it.

Without skipping a single battle on *Clash of Clans* or a stalking session on Google, observe yourself and take notes. You can use an app, keep track on your device, or go old school with a pen or pencil and notebook. The important thing is to accurately report how often you check your phone. What are you checking—e-mail, social media, missed phone calls, directions, the weather? Do you read on your phone? What do you read—those long e-mails from your mom, *The New York Times*, or hashtags on Instagram? When do you pull it out most? Or is it always in your hand, even while walking down the street, waiting on line, between appointments, or in transit? Are you alone or do you use it when you're in a meeting or with another person socially? Do you take it to the bathroom with you? These questions are just to get you thinking. Ask yourself whatever feels most relevant. The only requirement is that you answer honestly.

> *Don't* change your behavior as you track your digital usage.
> *Do* think about your goals for the Bored and Brilliant challenge, whether it's reading long novels again or making dinnertime a tech-free zone.

Take courage. When I tracked myself, my baseline numbers were pretty pathetic. My laptop, tablet, and phone know me better than anyone else. They know what I like and how to grab my attention.

I averaged around one hundred pickups of my phone *per day*. I also spent about seventy minutes responding to communications and using it.

Those harsh stats were right in line with most of the participants in the original Bored and Brilliant challenge. Among the 7,264 people who downloaded the app and signed up to participate in the project, the average usage was somewhere between ninety and one hundred minutes of phone time per day with forty to fifty pickups (when you just quickly check the screen for a text or new e-mail). (Friday was the biggest phone day, by the way, maybe because people were on Tinder.) Other researchers have estimated that the average American checks their phone 150 times per day. I hypothesized that our group started the project with far

Notes on Challenge One

"Love this challenge. Here's what I've noticed about myself on day one: it's very easy to keep the phone out of sight in the first half of the day, when I'm feeling fresh and energized and upbeat. By the time I reach the middle of the day, when I'm more stressed by deadlines and a million tasks pulling my attention in many directions, I feel frazzled and tired and have an impulse to go to my phone every five minutes— both to distract from tasks I don't want to finish and because I'm getting tired and want some kind of easy instant gratification rather than pushing through the hard tasks. So maybe that moment when we're challenged by stress and instinctively go to the phone is one to pay attention to."

—Paulo

"Just downloaded BreakFree for my phone! I love this idea. Let's stand around and do nothing and be super bored and even be in an elevator with other people awkwardly standing there."

—R.J.

fewer pickups due to greater self-awareness and motivation to change behavior.

How to Take the Challenge

First, download the Moment app (if you're an Apple user) or the Break-Free app (if you're an Android user). The app will guide you through specific steps to establish your baseline data. I recommend using an app over taking notes the old-fashioned way because it is more accurate. When I used Moment to track my own numbers, I could see I was reflexively checking my phone the minute I got into an elevator, a behavior I would not even have noticed enough to mark down manually. The digital tracking will allow you not only to see unconscious patterns but also to follow your progress throughout the week with hard numbers. Many people have joked about the irony of using an app for a project that is an attempt to regain control or put limits on technology. But as I said before, this book isn't anti-tech. We want to learn to live with it in a healthier way, so what better tool to use in that effort than technology itself?

Survey Yourself

Here are some questions to get you thinking more about how you use your devices. Your answers will help you get to know your digital habits better and figure out what information and tips will best help you find equilibrium.

1. Where do you generally keep your phone?
    a. On my desk
    b. In my pocket
    c. In my bag
    d. In my hand
    e. Other (please specify): _____

2. Overall, I think I spend _____ on my phone each day:
    a. Way too much time
    b. Too much time
    c. Just the right amount of time
    d. Not enough time
    e. No time

3. What are the top three apps that you open most frequently? Please rank each of these 1, 2, or 3, and feel free to enter a response you don't see listed below.
    a. Phone calls
    b. E-mail
    c. Texting
    d. Navigation
    e. Social media
    f. Camera
    g. Games
    h. Other (please specify): _____
    i. N/A

4. Part of this project is about rethinking where your phone and computer fit into your life. Which behaviors are you most interested in cutting down?
    a. Checking/opening
    b. Game playing
    c. Texting
    d. Talking
    e. Photo taking
    f. Social media usage
    g. Overall time spent
    h. Other (please specify): _____
    i. None

5. Is there a time of day when you most want to change your phone- or computer-usage habits?
    a. Early morning (5 A.M.–9 A.M.)
    b. Morning (9 A.M.–12 P.M.)
    c. Lunchtime (12 P.M.–2 P.M.)
    d. Late afternoon (2 P.M.–5 P.M.)
    e. Evening (5 P.M.–8 P.M.)
    f. Night (9 P.M.–12 A.M.)
    g. Late night (12 A.M.–4 A.M.)
    h. Weekends
    i. All of the above
    j. None of the above
    k. N/A

6. Thinking about your overall stress level, please indicate how your phone or computer (or both) fit in:
    a. *Adds* stress to my life
    b. *Alleviates* stress in my life
    c. Does not contribute to my stress level
    d. N/A

7. In the past week, thinking about the personal and professional projects and ideas in front of you, have you had enough time to sit and think?
    a. I have had more than enough time to sit and think
    b. I have had just enough time to sit and think
    c. I have not had enough time to sit and think
    d. N/A

3

Out of Sight

You can't depend on your eyes when your imagination is out of focus.

—*Mark Twain*

Our gadgets have taken on a personified, maybe even mammalian, quality: We swath them in expensive covers; keep them tucked close to our bodies; soothe them when they squawk; feel frantic when they are misplaced. One of my listeners described his phone as "a best friend who has all the best and worst qualities." Another equated his phone to a baby's binky. Codependency, anyone?

Our love for our smartphones and other digital devices will not be denied, but how does that symbiosis affect our analog relationships and offline responsibilities? For sure, technology has introduced some incredible new possibilities for human contact that no one could have imagined a few decades ago. The Internet brings together people from all over the world. Whether for democratic revolutions or support groups, those who would otherwise never have had a chance to connect find community. Then there are the ways it has radically changed dating and love. I'm not just talking Tinder here. In my research, I came across a service you can sign up for, Invisible Girlfriend, where you receive texts from a girlfriend or boyfriend of your own design. There are real humans (who are paid) writing the texts, but not necessarily, or hardly ever, the same person writing back each time. At first when I heard about this crowd-sourced romance, I judged the people who signed up for it. I thought, *My God, put yourself out there—just a little.* But then I spoke to a young man who used the service. He has cerebral palsy and is in a wheelchair. He can't get out a lot, and when he does, women don't think of him as a romantic interest. That changed my perspective. While this man was clear about the inherent flaws with Invisible Girlfriend, it allowed him more possibilities than he had without it.

Yet, as I learned more about how technology conditions us in subtle, even imperceptible ways, I found more evidence that our ability to focus on our work or books wasn't the only thing mutating; it was also growing harder to give our full attention to flesh-and-blood people.

Nearly all of us know the irritation that comes from spending time with someone who keeps checking his or her phone. I, for example, understand my brother's need to stay in touch with his on-site construction crews who might have urgent questions. He's a builder. It's what he does. But it drives me and my sister crazy when the three of us get together for some quality sibling time and he insists he can simultaneously text his team *and* contribute to our conversation. After placating us with some "uh-huh's" and "sure's," he'll take a deep sigh, finally put the phone away, and return to the tactile world. Then, always with a laugh, he'll say, "Wait, what? I missed that." Dude! Don't make me repeat myself. I'm a busy lady! Well, it turns out there's some science behind my brother driving me nuts with his texting.

In a study from 2014 called *The iPhone Effect: The Quality of In-Person Social Interactions in the Presence of Mobile Devices*, researchers at Virginia Tech found that the mere presence of a mobile device, even just lying there, seemingly benign on the kitchen counter, can lower the empathy exchanged between two friends. In a "naturalistic field experiment," one hundred pairs of people were assigned a ten-minute conversation and then observed from a distance. If people happened to have a mobile device in their hands or on the table, they were not told to put the phones away. And guess what? "It was found that conversations in the absence of mobile communication technologies were rated as significantly superior compared with those in the presence of a mobile device, above and beyond the effects of age, gender, ethnicity, and mood," the study noted. "People who had conversations in the absence of mobile devices reported higher levels of empathetic concern. Participants conversing in the presence of a mobile device who also had a close relationship with each other reported lower levels of empathy compared with pairs who were less friendly with each other."

This study echoes in my mind every time I grab coffee with a friend. I used to make sure I put my phone facedown. Now I'm sure to get it off the table entirely. Call me snooty, but I'd like to be able to rate the majority of my conversations as "superior."

The consequences for our social-emotional life in an age of "ubiquitous computing environments," as the study put it, are enormous. The history of humanity has proved that human beings find it hard enough already to forge relationships, build trust, and understand other perspectives. Why add yet another stumbling block in the form of a phone when in-person interaction is often limited these days anyway?

Talk versus Text

Work, parenting, dating (oh, dating)—texting leaves no realm untouched. Even when the messages become inane (think fifteen texts back and forth about who can be home to sign for a package when a one-minute call would settle it), many people still refuse to pick up the stupid phone. I see this tendency in the young radio producers I work with. They look freaked out when I suggest they call a source who hasn't responded to multiple e-mailed requests. They don't know how to do "good phone"— use their voice rather than the crafted written word to convince or cajole.

In a story about instant messaging with his twelve-year-old son for *The Moth*, *New Yorker* writer Adam Gopnik puzzled at younger generations' preference for writing to talking. Sending words rapidly versus hearing someone's voice in real time—for him it's about choosing the new rather than the better. "If Steve Jobs had invented the phone call, it would have been on the front page of the *Times* the next day, and there'd have been giant back-page ads everywhere you looked talking about 'Finally, real voices! Real communication! Liberate yourself from the pressure of the keyboard,'" Gopnik wrote. "It would have been the great breakthrough of the twentieth century. But because that was the nineteenth century, kids only instant message."

MIT professor Sherry Turkle has a different theory. The trained sociologist and clinical psychologist, whose previous book, *Alone Together*, topped the *New York Times* bestseller list, got the idea for her new book, *Reclaiming Conversation*, after hearing people say over and over that they'd rather text than talk. It was a sentiment she didn't understand and therefore wanted to investigate.

Turkle's research began with a simple question: What's wrong with conversation? One eighteen-year-old reflected what many others felt when she said, "I'll tell you what's wrong with conversation, it takes place in real time, and you can't control what you're going to say." Turkle was dumbfounded. That's exactly what she thought was *right* with conversation. "What's with us that we've gotten afraid of revealing ourselves to each other in the spontaneity of face-to-face talk?" she asked. Texting and messaging afford us the ability to edit ourselves and present what we imagine is a more "perfect" version of ourselves, Turkle explained.

This desire was also borne out in her work as an MIT professor when her students would rather e-mail her than come to office hours. When she asked them why, they again described the "perfect e-mail" in which they can refine and edit their issues into a finely honed request and then receive an equally optimal response and resolution. Turkle finds these transactions cold and limited by the medium. "Why I'm a professor and love learning is that in college somebody cared about me," Turkle said. "A professor said, 'You're smart, you can do it.' Or, 'Here's a bad idea, but together, we're going to make it better.' I can't do that if my students are writing me a perfect e-mail and I'm writing back a perfect e-mail. That's not where it's going to happen."

It's true—I learned early on in college that I'm one of those people who think best aloud, a trait I might never have discovered if a professor I had freshman year hadn't nodded encouragement at me in class as I incrementally built an argument about the economic repercussions of the French Revolution.

The university is a microcosm of our world, where human contact in all its inspirational and awkward messiness continues to shrink in the face of technological solutions. As Turkle writes in *Reclaiming Conver-*

sation, there is a program being developed at MIT where people type in their problems that in turn get sent to Amazon Mechanical Turk—a global online job forum where a crowd-sourced workforce engages in microlabor or assignments posted by "Requesters," which can range from taking surveys to color-coding shoes sold online to *therapy*. Freud would roll over in his grave at the talking cure 2.0, where one person hears about your recurring nightmare of a plane crashing and another in some other part of the world hears of your problems with your overbearing mother. Turkle's problem with outsourcing mental health care to anonymous virtual day laborers is that there's "no one person who's thinking through you and relating to you." And, I would add, working with you to find a potential solution.

Turkle sees virtual therapy and texting over talking as part of society's larger trend toward devaluing conversation and the "human sensibility." "We've forgotten that conversation is supposed to be with another person who can remember the previous conversation," she said. "Conversation happens because there is history and empathy." So much for eyes being the window to the soul.

Studies proving that the presence of a phone during a conversation deteriorates the quality of the exchange are just common sense, according to Turkle. (The Virginia Tech study was replicated with a phone not on the table in front of the participants talking but in the line of their peripheral vision—and it still had a big impact!) "If you're thinking you could be interrupted, you're not going to share something really intimate," Turkle said. "Even a silent phone disconnects us." One of the students Turkle interviewed for her book follows something she named the "Rule of Three" for this very reason. Three people have to have their heads up in the conversation in order for her to feel comfortable dropping out. Safe in the knowledge that the conversation is being sustained, only then will she put down her head and look at her phone.

Turkle is passionate about her mission to reclaim conversation not only for our personal well-being but also for the benefit of society at large. "Every generation needs the capacity to sustain a complicated conversation about complicated things," she said. "You can't solve difficult political or economic problems with a sound bite."

Unfortunately, something meta happens when Turkle's message about conversation and connection is condensed (think book blurb or tweet): It can come across as old-fashioned or fuddy-duddy rather than an evolved look at our relationship to technology. At the very least, her students, those who insist on finely crafting e-mails rather than visiting her during office hours, are now excellent writers. And if they can barely hold a conversation, well, all hope is not lost. Just as we have changed our brains, so can we change them back. "One of the things that's so extraordinary is how *resilient* we are," Turkle said. "It only takes five days at a summer camp without devices for the markers for empathy among young people to start to go right back up again. We are built to be empathic creatures, so it just takes a little to restore this balance."

There's just one problem: I doubt those MIT college kids (or you and I) are headed to a sleepaway camp where the only chirping is from crickets and not your phone. In fact, I admitted to Turkle that my husband and I text at least five to ten times a day, and I love it. We have a *great* texting relationship. His ten-word, funny, and self-deprecating messages distill him to the very essence of his personality, and on days when we barely get to see each other in person, these moments of contact seem really good for our relationship. Are they "superior" conversations? Well, no, but at least we are connecting as much as two busy professionals with children and crazy schedules can.

"I think that's *awesome*," Turkle replied. "My problem isn't with texting. My problem is texting when you are in the physical presence of another person." Just as I do in this book, she argues that her research is not anti-technology in the least. "I *love* texting. I *love* my phone," she said. "For somebody who grew up thinking that the most she would ever get was a Dick Tracy two-way wrist radio, my phone is a miracle! The problem is when you're dividing your attention between other people and your phone. Sometimes we have to give ourselves a chance to unfold to each other." Unfolding takes time, stutters and starts, embarrassing moments, and awkward pauses . . . conversational nuance the space bar can't help us with.

Touch Screens Can Change How We Perceive the World—Or at Least Make for Faster Thumbs

Our obsession with technology and the new intensive work we've found for our previously opposable yet undervalued thumbs is a neuroscientist's dream. All the tapping and swiping makes for neatly and accurately organized data for researchers studying the brain plasticity of ordinary people as they do everyday tasks—like texting. At least that's how Arko Ghosh, of the University of Zurich and ETH Zurich in Switzerland, and his colleagues felt when they began researching the connection between our digital use and brain activity.

By measuring the electrical activity in different parts of the brain in people who used smartphones compared to those using "dumbphones," the researchers found that the activity in the brain's cortex, which is associated with the thumb and index fingertips, was directly proportional to how much a person used her phone. That seems sort of obvious, but, as Ghosh told *Current Biology* when he published the study in January 2015, "I was really surprised by the *scale* of the changes."

Based on their electroencephalogram (EEG) readings, which monitored the electrical messages traveling between the brain and the hands, smartphone users had larger brain activity measurements when they used their thumb, index, and middle fingers. And the more they texted, the bigger the EEG response grew.

"Smartphone users have a brain that processes touch differently than people who don't use smartscreen touch phones," Ghosh told Reuters. This isn't much different from professional French horn players or surgeons for whom the part of their brain that corresponds to the fingers they use for work is larger than it is in the rest of us. Still, it's kind of freaky if you think about it: texting a lot is shaping our brains in new ways. For the better? While this study was confined to how our brain processes touch, I would answer yes. We are "better" at answering texts quickly on a teeny-tiny keyboard with pithy five-word retorts. All joking aside, this research raises questions about how smartphone use affects other areas of our brains that have yet to be studied.

Resisting the Reflex

Technology conforms to the age-old adage—there's a time and a place for everything. (Clichés. They're always true.) But how do we teach ourselves, and our children, self-regulation when it comes to this powerful stuff? When does a conversation require you to put the phone out of sight, not just facedown on the table in front of you? What if something truly urgent or an emergency situation arises while you are making a "human connection," and your family can't get hold of you? Or, as in the case of my colleague, who needs the phone to remotely let in the dog walker (during her therapy appointments, no less!).

Before I spiraled out of control with what-ifs, I got a reality check from Dr. Alex Soojung-Kim Pang, a tech forecaster, scholar at Stanford, and author of *The Distraction Addiction*. Pang's road to creating what he calls "contemplative computing" began after his very first mobile upgrade. Even futurists are susceptible to the siren call of the smartphone. Pang felt his ability to concentrate for long stretches of time in the lab slipping away. Projects started to pile up. There never seemed to be enough time in the day. Instead of high-level problem solving, he'd find himself looking at his damn phone. He began to panic.

"I went through my own crisis with all these technologies," he explained. "As a technology forecaster and futurist in Silicon Valley, I spend all my day online. Like most of us, I've got a lot of things going on simultaneously. There's not a lot of downtime. After a few years of doing it, I began to feel like I was losing my ability to really concentrate seriously."

This terrified Pang, who came to Silicon Valley via Oxford and other such ivory towers. He prized his ability to dive into dense documents and wrestle with complex, arcane ideas over long periods of time. Grappling with disparate ideas and finding solutions was not only vital to Pang's academic and financial success, it also deeply satisfied him. He thought of his intellect as an essential part of his makeup until he "felt that slipping away." In addition to the high-level thinking issues, he also experienced mundane memory trouble. "I would walk into a room to get something, and by the time I got there I would forget what I had gone to look for," he said.

Pang wasn't just starting to have "senior moments." Observing his own behavior more closely, he realized the little phone in his hand was tyrannizing his time and holding his brain hostage.

"Smartphones behave like a four-year-old child," Pang said. "Their default is set to alert you to absolutely everything." When a new text comes in, a little pop-up window appears. E-mail, a buzzing. WhatsApp. Snapchat. Bubbles everywhere, and the next thing you know, you are drowning.

Pang continued his smartphone-to-small-child analogy: "When they want your attention, they want it right now. They have no sense of social boundaries, that there are times when it's okay to interrupt you and there are times when it's not. If you let kids run wild, then they learn that it's perfectly okay to do that. But as parents, we can teach our kids better rules. Likewise, we can teach our smartphones better rules. We can turn them from devices that constantly interrupt us into devices that protect our attention."

Armed with the firm belief that "distraction is a choice," Pang set about researching and developing more mindful digital practices that could transform our phones from unruly brats to well-behaved tots; ways we can set up and use our devices that "puts them in their place." Our devices aren't going anywhere; they are a permanent part of the modern world. Still, that doesn't mean distraction has to be.

Just as we discovered during the Bored and Brilliant Project, Pang also found that his productivity required time for mind-wandering or, as he put it, to "do nothing at all." Sorry—there's no skipping the step between emptying your e-mail in-box and coming up with your next business idea.

For Pang, this meant getting back to his academic roots and attacking the literature on the neuroscience and psychology of attention, multitasking, and other forms of self-distraction that affect the brain. "And I also started meditating," he said. "I am probably the world's worst meditator."

I insisted he was in serious competition with me for that title. But Pang says when it comes to meditation, "even when you do it badly, you get benefit from it." In exploring contemplative practices as part of his goal of restoring his mental acuity, he realized that the tools developed in Buddhism and other traditions to confront the conundrum of existence were also "solutions to problems that we confront every time we switch on our phone or our tablet computer or sit down and open up Facebook and Twitter."

It makes sense. Just as yoga can get us to be more present in our bodies, so can applying a mindfulness practice help us be more, well, mindful about how we use our gadgets. Let's use the word "purposeful." As a society, we have decided—much like our beloved devices—it's either *on* or *off.* You know, the parents who don't let their kids have any screen time versus those who believe kids should have unlimited access to *Minecraft* because it's creative. Does it have to be either an appreciation of all the optimization tech has to offer *or* going on some sort of digital Sabbath? Is it possible to have a healthy relationship with our tech? Or is consistent vigilance just too taxing?

In researching his book, Pang did spend time with those who turn off anything with a screen or social media sites (from one day a week to once a month). He also supports taking these kinds of breaks if they help people be more conscious and conscientious in their use of technology. The whole point of what he calls "contemplative computing" is the integration of these best practices into our digital life. Not having no life at all. "Just as the solution to stress at work is not necessarily to quit your job but to learn how to deal with it better, so too can we come up with ways of interacting with our devices—or ways that they interact with *us*—to avoid a lot of these problems," he said.

Pang isn't alone in making mindfulness work for the Information Age. There is a whole market for "Zenware," software programs that do anything from manage the typical clutter on personal computers to meditation apps to a plug-in that turns your Internet off. An entire subset of this Zenware strips down computer programs to their barest utility (think no pull-down menus) so you can "confront the existential terror of the blank page rather than spend most of your time playing around with formatting and macros and doing all the other things that you can do with complicated programs that feel like work but really aren't that productive."

On the Zen tech front, Pang discovered a community of Buddhist monks and nuns who are "avid social media users." They blog, tweet, update their status, and hold online meditation sessions. The mind-set of these modern monks blew him away, because they don't see a division between virtual and physical reality. For them, all realities are the same. Pang understood this when he asked them how it was they spent so much time online without losing their ability to focus (or their center), which happens to so many of the rest of us. "Half of them didn't even understand the question," he said. "It was like asking someone, 'How is it that you're able to eat food in a gravitational field?'"

Still, the monks and nuns considered Pang's query and after a while returned to him with an answer in the form of another question: "Why is it that you think that technologies are any more distracting than your own mind or anything else in the world?"

Distraction doesn't come from devices or people or things, they posited. It is an internal problem.

That stripped-down and, in a way, scary answer inspired Pang. If the problem is internal, that means no matter how fast technology is moving around us, the solution lies inside us as well. "Even if we are living in a world populated by weapons of mass distraction, technologies that are finely crafted to get us to spend as much time with them as possible so that they can sort of learn as much about us as they can and take that data and resell it to advertisers," Pang said, "even in that kind of world, we still are able to reach within ourselves and come up with ways of dealing with these devices that work well for us."

Pang's Four Steps to Good Phone Hygiene

Mastering our screen time is a skill like meditation, public speaking, or even *World of Warcraft*. The devices we rely upon to stay connected and productive can take on an "inevitable" quality—we feel required to pay attention to them. But what Pang wants everyone to know is that you can "make choices about the role that these technologies play in your life." Here are Pang's prescriptions for putting that iPhone in its place (or at least making our lives with it a little more balanced):

1. Turn off nonvital notifications

Remember, when you first get any mobile device, it will behave like a child who wants all your attention all the time. "All their defaults are set to alert you to absolutely everything," said Pang, who turns off every notification for virtually everything on his phone and removes nonessential apps. "I have found that just accessing Facebook and Twitter from my laptop turns out to be perfectly fine."

2. Make sure you do get the notifications that matter to you

Ask yourself this important question: In an emergency—like the zombie apocalypse, say—whom do you want to be able to reach you? In Pang's case, it's his children's school, his immediate family, and a few close friends. To everyone on that list, he's assigned a specific ringtone—the opening bars of the Derek and the Dominos tune "Layla." "Even though I've heard that guitar lick a billion times, no matter where I am, it cuts through whatever I'm doing and I notice it," he said. "There are about a dozen people who get that ringtone. The rest of the world gets Brian Eno's *Ambient 1: Music for Airports*." No comment on Eno—it's just that "Layla" gets Pang to take notice, no matter how deep in concentration he is (and allows him to tune out anything else). He believes a phone should act like a good receptionist, who can decide whether a call needs to be answered immediately or it's better to take a message. Creating a white list, a small but sacred list of your priority people, and playing around with the ringtones "keeps you connected to the people who matter most to you, and the rest of the world at arm's length."

3. Fight phantom gadget syndrome

For people who don't know PGS, it's when you sense your phone is buzzing even when it's not. Okay, phantom gadget syndrome doesn't have its own acronym—yet—but most of you have probably experienced it. And it's freaky. I'll sheepishly admit that I often mistake my grumbling stomach for an incoming text. "We become so accustomed to extending our senses for the next call or next tweet, we begin to misinterpret other things," Pang says. Medical residents tend to have this symptom a lot, according to Pang, because if they miss their pager going off, it could possibly be the difference between life and death. Pang's prescription against this unnerving side effect of constant connection is to physically disconnect from your phone. Unless you are a doctor or belong to any other profession in which seconds really matter, he suggests not carrying your phone right against your body. Put it in a bag to create some boundaries and "tip the balance of your relationship with your phone back in your favor."

4. Remember to breathe

The message "Remember to breathe" is Pang's screen saver. Tech writer Linda Stone coined the term "e-mail apnea," which she defined as the "temporary absence or suspension of breathing, or shallow breathing, while doing e-mail." You know the feeling: when checking e-mail or waiting for a page to load, often we hold our breath (not to mention keep our shoulders hitched up to our ears). Pang explained that holding one's breath is an evolutionary signal of anxiety. "It's what you did a thousand years ago when you thought you were being stalked by a tiger and you needed to be really quiet," he said. Because of that, holding one's breath is an "unconscious stressor." Considering how many times most of us check our devices each day, that's a lot of stress. Putting a reminder to breathe on his locked screen means Pang sees the message dozens of times a day. And exhales. *Namaste*.

CHALLENGE TWO: Keep Your Devices out of Reach While in Motion

In one of my conversations with boredom expert Sandi Mann, she told me about some intriguing self-experimentation she did during her morning commute. She drives about an hour each way to work, and although she isn't checking her phone, Mann usually does have the radio on the entire time. One day, though, she decided to "switch it off and just let [her] mind wander." She continued to ride without any kind of media distraction. "By the end of my journey, I've usually come up with an idea for a study or for a book or how to redecorate my house or anything," she reports. It was classic autobiographical planning or future thinking—and, according to Mann, "it's actually quite refreshing."

I was struck by Mann's experiment and Pang's advice not to carry the phone on one's body but in a bag—both limit access to devices during a simple, straightforward, and clearly demarcated period: while in transit.

The idea is that when you are on the bus or walking down the street, you're not doing *nothing*. Actually, I should say, your mind is not doing *nothing*. We think of those moments as unproductive, inefficient, or lost if we're not checking our mail or doing other tasks. But these are ideal times for letting our minds wander.

So, your second challenge in the Bored and Brilliant Project is to keep your phone out of view (and not listen to headphones, either) anytime you are in transit. Whether driving, taking the bus, or just walking down the street, make it a completely tech-free time.

After Challenge One, perhaps you've begun to take notice of some of your own digital habits—habits that might have become so reflexive that you didn't even realize you were doing them. I, for example, have a tendency to walk down the street with my phone gripped tightly in my hand. Just in case I might need it. A clenched hand surely does not equal a wandering mind. If you are like me, you might want to ease into this challenge by putting your phone in your pocket. Overachievers can move straight to the bag. Just so long as any device is out of line of sight, it's okay. Look at it only when you have reached your destination.

"In motion" can be small motions, too. The first group of Bored and Brilliant participants included a stay-at-home mom with four-month-old twins and a two-and-a-half-year-old. She wasn't sure how she'd manage this particular challenge since, as she put it, "I spend a lot of time nursing on the couch, and don't get much farther than that." Our team at *Note to Self* told her that walking from the crib to the fridge absolutely counted as a commute. Here's what she reported back: "I decided to keep my phone on my table beside the couch, like a station, and in my diaper bag if I left the house," she said. "It worked. By 6 P.M., I only clocked forty-three minutes of phone time. This is *huge* for me!" As every busy mom knows, sometimes the only things you don't have to share with your children are your thoughts, so her realization definitely counts as a breakthrough for this mom. You don't know mental claustrophobia until you've gone to the toilet with a baby still on your lap. Parents, you know what I'm talking about.

Take a note from this intrepid mom and adapt Challenge Two to fit whatever constitutes traveling for you. The point of this exercise is to make every pickup purposeful.

Challenge Upgrade

During your usual commute to work or a route you take every day, take the time rescued from not looking at your phone and note five things you've never noticed before. It could be ornamental cornices and gargoyles (like the ones in my neighborhood that I never saw before I began strolling my colicky son around) or the way the light hits the clouds in the sky. It could also be details that are a lot less poetic, like a gorgeous pair of shoes in a store window that would go perfectly with a dress you just bought or simply another human being smiling at you.

When we did this challenge with the original Bored and Brilliant group, some of my listeners were so anxious about being separated from their tech, they needed to take baby steps. They practiced first by leaving their phones on their desks when they went to the bathroom.

Others, like Moira, another stay-at-home mother of two in New York City, took issue with the whole exercise. "My smartphone *is* my office," she explained. "'In transit' is my work time, not my downtime to do boredom scanning." Not so fast, Moira. See, her assumption was that she only checked her phone for efficient reasons such as weather updates or bus schedules.

Later, when Moira tracked her usage accurately, she got a vastly different picture of her relationship to her phone compared with the one she had in her head. Here's what she discovered:

- Quick e-mail checks while in the elevator (when she had just checked inside the apartment . . . and if she was just going downstairs to use the gym in the basement of her building, she checked her e-mail again while riding back up the elevator)
- *Candy Crush* binges that often lasted through her younger child's entire nap time, after which she found herself scrambling to get a snack made and pick up her elder child on time
- Once out the door with the stroller, there's always the quick twitch to check her phone for texts, e-mails, and other updates

After taking a good hard look at how she really engaged with technology, Moira decided to put the device down more often. She wasn't secretary of state. She didn't need to look at her phone on the walk home or in between errands. (She could check the weather *before* she left the house.) During the Bored and Brilliant week, Moira challenged herself to change her behavior. "When I jumped off the treadmill and headed back upstairs, I instinctively went to check my phone," she said. "But this time I caught myself. There were more lapses, but by the end of the week, I was catching it faster and putting the phone in the bag! It was a win when I walked all the way to school pickup without checking my phone."

Why was keeping her phone in her bag "a win"? Because, despite being initially skeptical of the whole idea of this challenge, Moira felt a burden lift when she stopped checking her phone so much. She reported being not only more productive with her time but also more in tune with her "children's musings." In a word, she found the experience "wonderful." By setting simple boundaries, Moira got immediate and powerful results.

According to the original Bored and Brilliant sample group, people who kept their phones stashed away and off their bodies averaged eighteen fewer minutes of general usage and eleven fewer pickups per day. Now, this is correlation, not causation. But there is obviously a connection between being a handholder (a small group in the bunch) and logging the most time and number of checks.

Where do you keep your phone?	Average minutes per day	Average pickups per day
In my bag	81	28
On my desk	89	37
In my pocket	88	45
In my hand	108	46
Other	112	31

I remember the first day I decided not to use my phone at all during my commute to work on the subway. That rainy morning, I went hard core: zero smartphone interaction, podcasts or otherwise. I read *the paper* (an article I'd printed out the night before—sorry, tree) instead. How did it feel? Not good at first. Like a lot of my listeners, I was uneasy kicking the scrolling habit and, at first, found the sensation distracting rather than focusing (how ironic). But after struggling for a few subway stops, I settled down and read the article all the way through, instead of the usual fits and starts over days, if not weeks. The result? More analysis and understanding of the story. (It was about Tom Brady's mental acuity, and I'm not even a football fan.) When I finally looked up from my reading, I let my mind go . . . and smelled the wet umbrellas, contemplated how applicable sports psychology is to the office, felt gratitude toward my husband for buying me new boots, and reminded myself to plan better for the next seasonal change. (No longer would I be the mom whose kids are still wearing sneakers in January!) Most important, though, when I arrived at work, I was decidedly less frantic. More calmly than usual, I checked my phone—for exactly *three minutes*. I didn't surf around. Instead, I got down to editing that week's episode without rushing. And it felt good.

Notes on Challenge Two

"I was bored, I guess. So I suddenly looked at the stairway that went to the top of the [subway] station and thought, *You know, I just came down that stairway but I could go back up and then come back down and get a little cardio.* So I did."

—Rachel

"As a graduate student, I spend a lot of my time either at a desk or driving. Therefore, on top of waiting to get to my destination to take out my phone, I decided to extend the challenge a little further and wait until I was done with some kind of assignment before checking e-mail, Facebook, or Instagram. Without my phone pulling me in so many different directions, I was stunned at how much better I understood the material (and with less effort). I was able to concentrate better on what I was doing and felt so relaxed when I was done."

—Ayana

"Making this a habit would definitely necessitate the purchase of a wristwatch at some point."

—Kara

4

Making Memories

*All photographs are memento mori. To take a
photograph is to participate in another
person's (or thing's) mortality, vulnerability,
mutability. Precisely by slicing out this moment and freezing it, all photographs testify
to time's relentless melt.*

—Susan Sontag

Boredom and mind-wandering are part of a day's work for Greg Colon.
As a security guard at the Guggenheim, he spends his eight-hour shifts
pacing around the New York City museum's galleries. His job is to make
sure visitors don't get too close to the art and to direct them to the latest
Fauvist exhibition. Sure, Saturdays in December are hectic, but Greg
also has a lot of downtime. Hours in his starched uniform, walking very
slowly, hands resting behind his back, from one room to another and
then back again, with only one or two or maybe no patrons to keep him
company. How does he manage to stay awake? By communing with his
other colleagues: the artwork. Thanks to those hours spent alone, with
just the canvases for company, Greg's discovered that he, too, has a creative eye. From a Philip Guston painting reminiscent of ice on a win-
dowpane to the flag of New Mexico on a visitor's tote bag oddly mimicked
in a work by Rauschenberg, art and life are deeply intertwined for Colon.
Beyond developing an aesthetic appreciation and deep relationship with
the art, Colon finds solace in the images on the wall.

"Your mind goes to different places that you don't even want it to go to sometimes," said Colon of the work of a museum guard, which he's been doing for the last fifteen years. "You might be thinking of problems, so then you try to get away from that by meditating, praying, just looking at the paintings." Truly the best museums embrace this secular calm, inviting you to test and recharge your mind.

Lately, though, something has been intruding on the reflective atmosphere that makes museums a special experience: smartphones.

"All I see is people getting on these gadgets, and it drives me crazy," said Colon, who leaves his cell phone at home when he's at work. "Sometimes they're not even looking at the paintings. They're just scrolling away."

The phenomenon is relatively new. In the early days of the technology, Colon remembered visitors self-policing, frowning at or even asking people who had their phone out to check e-mail or take selfies in the gallery to put it away. "Now you would look like a fool if you said something like that," he said.

That's especially true because the main way a lot of museumgoers seem to look at art these days is *through* their smartphones. While photography once was forbidden, many museums like the Guggenheim now permit snapping pictures of, well, pictures, except when otherwise noted in special exhibitions. Head into any major institution of art—the Met, the Prado, the Louvre (you can't even see the *Mona Lisa* at the Louvre because there are too many people taking pictures of it)—and it's like you're standing in front of Niagara Falls instead of a nude by Picasso. This holds true even at the 9/11 Memorial Museum in Downtown Manhattan.

Of course, the phenomenon of obsessive photo taking is not restricted to museums. Restaurants, fireworks displays, the bathroom—it seems every location is worth capturing at every moment. Park rangers, like those at Montana's Glacier National Park, now have a new danger to contend with in cell phones. "We see a lot of crazy stuff up there. People getting way too close, trying to take pictures, or surrounding a goat with a kid on the outside running around crying, trying to get to Mom, but, you know, there's fifteen people around Mom taking a picture," park ranger Mark Biel told *Morning Edition*. "That's kind of unacceptable."

Not even goats in the most remote wilderness can escape our contemporary photomania.

STAGGERING DIGITAL-PHOTO STATS
- Americans take more than 10 billion photos every month.
- Seventy-five percent of all photos are now taken with a phone.
- Snapchat users share 8,796 photos every second. (WhatsApp clocks in at 8,102 photos per second, and Facebook at 4,501 per second.)
- In 2014, people uploaded an average of 1.8 billion digital images every day (up from 500 million photos a day in 2013) for a total of 657 billion photos per year.

The explosive proliferation of digital images is one of the most fascinating, pervasive, and least manageable aspects of contemporary life. Not only have we decided to capture a significant portion of our lives with the expectation that we can experience it all over again later on Instagram, but our obsession with snapping has also launched a massive industry devoted to photo filters, archiving, and managing our memories (and yet we still don't know where those pictures of the trip to Miami are). It's also led to even more art. For his project *24 Hrs in Photos*, the Dutch artist Erik Kessels downloaded every photo uploaded to Flickr in one day, printing out 350,000 of about a million uploads that he heaped like enormous snowdrifts that reached from the gallery's floor to the ceiling. As Kessels told *The New York Times Magazine* in 2015, "I visualize the feeling of drowning in representations of other people's experiences." Are we indulging in visual gluttony?

The very nature of photography is changing at a rate of millions of images per second. For many of us, photography was rare and special, a way to document beauty or a milestone. I think of my mother-in-law, who, despite having the latest iPhone, still lines us up for big smiles. Those artificial poses take me right back to the days when finishing a roll of thirty-six frames meant a trip to the drugstore and shelling out another twenty dollars.

Now, thanks to smartphones, the very purpose of photographs has morphed into a powerful and speedy mode of information sharing. In the survey we did of the original Bored and Brilliant participants, teenagers reported that they couldn't imagine a day without taking and posting pictures. Photos are "the primary way that we keep in touch," one respondent said, echoing the sentiments of many. As another put it, "I would feel very lonely without taking or receiving photos." It's not about creating a memory . . . these photos have an underlying message, saying, "I'm thinking of you" or "Look at me" or "Isn't this fruit salad gorgeous?" They are an invitation to conversation. Sort of.

In an essay on the new "fabric of photos," the tech writer Om Malik explains the elements that make this proliferation possible, including unlimited bandwith, storage, and high-quality cameras built into our devices. He uses his niece, who always keeps Snapchat open to share every few minutes, as an example of the "generation [that] has never felt any constraints." In a conversation Malik had with Peter Neubauer, cofounder of Neo Technology and the open-source database Neo4j, the Swedish tech leader predicted a fundamental shift in the importance of photography from an individual to a collaborative endeavor. "Photos have always been tools of creative, artistic, and personal satisfaction," Malik wrote. "But going forward, the real value creation will come from stitching together photos as a fabric, extracting information and then providing that cumulative information as a totally different package."

Heady stuff. For now, however, the pictures filling the cloud are mainly from people documenting every angle of themselves and their lives. I mean, come on, those vacation sunsets, children on their first day of school, and farm-to-table entrées aren't going to take pictures of themselves! It can be hard to parse the line between capturing and holding dear a fleeting impression of precious life and immediately jumping mentally ahead to what people are going to think when they see your amazing photo. Your daughter is gorgeous. Your peaches and cream look like they came right out of *Real Simple*. Your taste is exquisite; your life is sublime. Right?

As gratifying (or soul-destroying) as crafting an idealized narrative of oneself on social media can be, let's not dismiss the time-suck aspect. In her research, Sherry Turkle came across a common theme that can be exemplified by the story of one father. This well-intentioned dad signed up for a school field trip in an effort to get closer to his daughter, but he wound up spending the entire trip, starting with the bus ride, taking pictures, posting them to Facebook, and, naturally, tracking his likes—that is, until his daughter pointed out that he hadn't spoken to her in over an hour.

When Turkle told me this story, my first thought was that a father posting pictures of his daughter on Facebook is in itself a form of intimacy. He's making sure that his wife, grandparents, friends, the whole world knows that it was worth taking the day off from work to spend with his daughter. He's including them in the outing, letting them also enjoy the squeamish glee on his daughter's face when she attempts to milk a cow. Isn't that worthwhile? Isn't it generous?

Turkle doesn't believe that kind of public attention makes up for what the daughter really wants—for her father to pay attention to *her*. "Over and over again, I heard the same thing from kids, the generation that theoretically loves technology," she said. "'Dad, please stop Googling. Mom, stop checking your phone. I just want to talk to you.' That was repeated in different forms, by so many different people."

To prove the importance of unmediated interaction, Turkle cited a famous set of experiments, known as the Still Face Experiments. In the 1970s, the developmental and clinical psychologist Edward Tronick observed infants in this series of face-to-face interactions with their mothers: a normal interaction to provide a baseline; a "still-face" section where the adult keeps a neutral expression and is unresponsive to the infant; and, lastly, a return to the normal interaction between mother and child. In describing the effects of the three-minute interaction with an unresponsive mother on the infant, Tronick said the baby "rapidly sobers and grows wary. He makes repeated attempts to get the interaction into its usual reciprocal pattern. When these attempts fail, the infant withdraws [and] orients his face and body away from his mother with a withdrawn, hopeless facial expression."

The Still Face Phenomenon, or SFP, has been replicated more than eighty times (one of the most successful rates in developmental psychology) in a range of related experiments, which have found associations between SFP and future adaptation of babies in terms of issues with behavior and attachment.

"It's crazy-making to face another human being and be ignored," Turkle puts it bluntly. "It's toxic for children, but even as adults, it's hard to tolerate someone we're trying to relate to showing so little empathy that they literally just turn away and look at something else as though we're not trying to connect with them. And we're doing that to each other now all the time. That's our new social norm."

Turkle rails that it's time for us to rethink this dynamic and turn our attention away from our devices and back toward the people with whom we want to have a relationship. Turkle would disapprove of my recent behavior at the playground. My kid looked so adorable in her Yankees cap and sundress, I wanted to remember her like that forever. "Let me take a picture of you," I asked for perhaps the third time that outing. Ever the obliging model, my daughter cycled through a range of facial expressions for me and my phone. (Normal! Kooky! Sad!) And then she asked to look at them. Instead of giving the monkey bars another try, we both looked at my phone on a stunning September afternoon. Blech. But here's my excuse: It's hard to be vigilant when the need to capture and bottle up beauty surrounds us. So I'm trying to limit myself and take pictures of her once a day instead of all day long. I know she's growing up and life is fleeting. But pictures aren't going to help me cope with an existential crisis down the road. My goal is to be in the moment more often than photographing it.

Beauty Is in the "Likes"

Shankar Vedantam, who explores social science research on his podcast, *Hidden Brain*, reported on an interesting experiment regarding the effect social media has on our brains—more specifically, our evaluation of the images we see on it.

UCLA's Lauren Sherman wanted to test out the theory that young people's brains work differently on Twitter and Instagram than they do in the physical world. "Suddenly, there are these interactions that have a little number on them, whether it's a like or a retweet or a favorite," she said in Vedantam's report on *Morning Edition*. "And I was really curious how that quantifiable interaction was affecting the way that teens perceived information online."

So she and her colleagues scanned the brains of adolescents as they looked at a simulated Instagram feed of pictures by the subjects and their "friends" (really, the researchers). The results were that the more likes a photo had, the more activity it generated in the nucleus accumbens—part of the brain's reward center. Even when researchers played around with the likes—giving the same picture fifty likes for one subject and five for another—it didn't matter. The number of likes was the determining factor in stimulating the part of the brain that makes you feel good.

For anyone who knows a fourteen-year-old or once was one, the fact that their tastes are guided by peer pressure isn't particularly surprising. Still, the implications for young people's sense of self in relation to posting and perusing pictures are unsettling. "The remarkable thing is that this was also true of the photos that the teenagers had taken themselves," Vedantam said. "Rather than make up their own minds about which of their own pictures they liked, teens deferred to the opinions of their peers."

The Photo-Taking Impairment Effect

When it comes to obsessional tech habits, photo taking probably isn't the worst on the list for relationships. If you're not gazing into someone's eyes, at least you're pointing an iPhone at them. But how does that persistent need to capture the moment, which so many of us feel, change how we actually *experience* the moment—both in the present and when we try to recall it down the line? The answer is quite illuminating.

One of the major reasons we take photos in the first place is to remember a moment long after it has passed—the birth of a baby, a reunion, a pristine lake. In the Bored and Brilliant survey, many adults said they used photos as a "memory aid," taking pictures of things like parking spots or the label of the hot sauce at a restaurant to buy later. But every time we snap a quick pic of something, it could in fact be harming our memory of it.

Linda Henkel, a professor of psychology at Fairfield University, studied how taking photos impacts experience and memory by crafting an experiment using a group of undergraduates on a guided tour of the university's Bellarmine Museum of Art. The students were asked to take photos of objects they looked at on the tour and simply observe others. The next day, she brought all the subjects into her research lab to test their memory of all the objects they had seen on the tour. Whenever they remembered a piece of work, she asked follow-up questions on specific visual details.

The results were clear—people remembered fewer of the overall objects they had photographed. They also couldn't recall as many specific visual details of the photographed art as compared to the art they had merely observed. "When you take a photo of something, you're counting on the camera to remember for you," Henkel said. "You're basically saying, 'Okay, I don't need to think about this any further. The camera's captured the experience.' You don't engage in any of the elaborative or emotional kinds of processing that really would help you remember those experiences, because you've outsourced it to your camera."

In short, if your camera captures the moment, then your brain doesn't. Henkel came up with a frightening term for this phenomenon. She calls her findings the "photo-taking-impairment effect."

Okay, okay. Of course you'd remember things better if you were completely in the present, hyperaware of every detail, like some supreme Zen master. But isn't that what photos are for? To refresh our fallible memories? Henkel doesn't disagree on the basic premise that the purpose of outsourcing our memory to devices frees up our brains to do other cognitive processing. The problem is, Henkel says, "We're constantly going from one thing to the next to the next." Instead of outsourcing so we can focus our attention on more important tasks, "we have this constant stream of what's next, what's next, what's next and never fully embrace any of the experiences we're having."

Nonetheless, Henkel and her student Katelyn Parisi ran another study to see what happens to memory when people have photos to remind them of a moment or object. (Although, in the real world, Henkel rightly observes, "We're so busy capturing photos, afterwards we don't actually look at them, because we have hundreds and thousands of them." Who hasn't dumped a bunch of photos of a graduation or trip into Dropbox and promised to make an album only to never ever look at them again?)

This time when people took a tour of the museum, they were asked to take two kinds of photos—those of the objects in the exhibit alone and others while standing next to objects. Afterward, Henkel had the subjects look at all the photos and then interviewed them on their memories of what they saw. "It turns out that it actually changes your perspective on the experience, whether you're in a photo of it or not," Henkel said. If you are in the image, you become more removed from the original moment. It is as if you are an observer watching yourself doing something outside yourself. Whereas if you are *not* in the image, you return to the first person, reliving the experience through your own eyes.

How taking pictures affects our understanding of ourselves and the things we are taking pictures of is still a big question mark. But as a result of her experiments, there is one thing Henkel is sure of. "Cameras, as amazing as they are, can't compare to what the brain is capable of with input from the eyes and the ears," Henkel said. "Cameras are a lesser version of the human information-processing system."

HOW TO TAKE A PHOTO TO ENHANCE YOUR MEMORY
Even if you can't bear to face a computer hard drive that's nightmarishly filled with photos, in Henkel's experiments, there was one way in which taking pictures did *not* erode people's memories. Back on that tour of the art museum, "When participants zoomed in to photograph a specific part of the object, their subsequent recognition and detail memory was not impaired, and, in fact, memory for features that were not zoomed in on was just as strong as memory for features that were zoomed in on," the professor wrote in her study. "This suggests that the additional attention and cognitive processes engaged by this focused activity can eliminate the photo-taking-impairment effect." I believe the science, and a bunch of close-ups of toes, noses, and brushstrokes would make for a pretty weird Instagram feed.

CHALLENGE THREE: Photo-Free Day

Your instructions: See the world through your eyes, not your screen. Take absolutely no pictures today. Not of your lunch, not of your children, not of your cubicle mate, not of that beautiful sunset. No picture messages. No cat pics. Instagrammers, it's gonna get rocky. Snapchatsters? Hang in there. Everyone is going to be okay. I promise.

Those of you, like my mother, who take one picture a month will find this challenge a breeze. But don't be smug. Your tough day is coming. And this might be harder than you think. Just as they did when refraining from looking at the phone in transit, many people reported that they took pictures way more (and way more mindlessly) than they had previously imagined. There will be rewards for your sacrifice. "Sure, the world *does* want to see my adorable grandchildren and gorgeous children," Beth in Indiana wrote us. "However, it's been a liberating twenty-four hours!"

While there are no Bored and Brilliant challenge winners, if someone were to claim that prize for take-no-photo day, it might have to be Vanessa Jean Herald, whose green Subaru skidded off the highway and into a snowy ditch during her one-hour commute between the southern Wisconsin farm where she lives and her job in Madison. Although she had to wait more than two hours in frigid temperatures for a tow truck to arrive, Herald did not lose her Bored resolve! "I placed my necessary emergency calls, sent some texts to let folks know I was okay, and then just sat," she wrote. "Sure, my gut reaction was to snap a picture of the car sitting in the ditch and covered with thrown snow for Instagram. Or to snap a photo of the cool way the red and blue lights of the sheriff's car blinked in my rearview mirror and lit up the roadway as the day turned to night through my two-hour mandatory break from life. But thanks to today's challenge, instead, I chilled out, took it all in, and then pulled out my writing notebook to jot down a story about how the best-laid plans sometimes end you up in a ditch on the side of the road." [Place imaginary photo of green Subaru in a snowy ditch on the side of the road here.]

Don't worry if your photo-free inspiration doesn't spill out in the shape of a well-formed story. It's okay to be uncomfortable, hostile, or, hopefully, bored without photos to fill your day. Just use your brain instead of your phone. No one is going to "heart" or "like" whatever goes on up there—except for you.

CHALLENGE UPGRADE
Now, if you really want a digital-image detox, avoid all photo proliferation—meaning you can check out images on social media, but don't "like" or retweet them. Just take a good hard look . . . and maybe a mental picture.

Notes on Challenge Three

"Ahh, today's Bored and Brilliant challenge is taking no photos!! I'm getting my cattoo today. Yup! A cat tattoo! Blast my timing. Had my Instagram caption planned for weeks. Will ask a friend to take a pic instead. Is that cheating?"

—Min

"I only made it to 4:30 P.M. and had to take a screenshot. I'm sorry but I saw the worst Tinder about me and I couldn't help it."

—Raina

"I'm not one to take daily photos on my phone, but dammit, today my toddler was doing something so cute (hiding under a bunch of paper bags even though I could clearly still see him with his head turned facing away from me), and I resisted taking a picture. Tomorrow I'll tell my kid not to do anything cute."

—Rochelle

"I had wondered why my sense of self and imagination had started to feel watered down over the last year.... I'm feeling as if I'm awakening from an extended mental hibernation. I hope this isn't premature excitement over a sudden sense of 'control,' but damn if it doesn't feel good."

—David

5

App Addled

*The shower has become one of the few
sacred spaces that we have without technology. For now.*

—Golden Krishna

It was a typical night in my house, kids tucked up in bed, nice and quiet—and I was ready to get my fix.

I felt at once excited and just plain pathetic. If I was honest with myself, I had been looking forward to this moment all day. And yet I hated being beholden to this . . . *game*?

Yes, that's right. Me, a working mother of two who complains constantly about having so much to do. I can't even think straight, couldn't stop playing a stupid mobile game. My vice? A puzzle app called *Two Dots*; like *Candy Crush*, but prettier. Think of it as the digital game equivalent of artisanal pickles made in Brooklyn.

I had never been into games (I think I'm the only person who went to college in the '90s and *didn't* play *Tetris*), but I had decided to download *Two Dots* as part of an investigation into how people get hooked on games. For research. Like a reporter who tries heroin so she can understand the crime beat.

For people who haven't fallen under its spell, let me explain the gist of *Two Dots*. The simplest game you can imagine, it's basically a grid of dots in various colors that you connect by drawing a line between any two of the same color. Just reading that sentence makes it sound boring.

But those tiny balls wanted so badly to be brought together with my index finger. They beckoned me with their gleeful bouncing on the screen. "We need you!" they seemed to call. They were friendly. Once connected . . . they were so soothing. It didn't take long for me to get hooked. Soon I was playing *Two Dots* on my commute home (and missing my stop), waiting in the dentist's office, and after putting my kids to bed—when I should have been contemplatively listening to their breathing and making sense of my hectic day. Okay, that's not realistic. How about at least talking to my husband over a glass of wine. Or at least not staying up hours after I should have been asleep or learning a new language or doing yoga or anything other than connecting those stupid dots!

I had to face it: *Two Dots* turned into the monkey on my back, my one-too-many scotch and sodas. The need to play was keeping me from doing basic things like reading, communicating, thinking, and relaxing. I wanted to understand how I got like this—how this app managed to suck me in and then keep a tight grasp over me. Because I knew I wasn't alone in my problem.

Flurry Analytics—a nearly universal tool used by app developers to track user data over billions of smart devices—reported that from 2014 to 2015, "worldwide mobile addicts grew 59 percent." While "regular users" (people who use apps between once and sixteen times daily) saw a 25 percent increase and "super users" (those who use apps between seventeen and sixty times daily) went up 34 percent, "mobile addicts," which they define as consumers who launch applications upward of *sixty times per day*, were the fastest-growing group by far. Even the mobile analytics company, which has been tracking usage since 2005, was caught off guard by this statistic. "It is actually hard to believe that Mobile Addicts are now 280 million strong," the report stated.

Even if you aren't hitting apps sixty times a day, just about everyone has one particular app—that one damn app—that steals away time from unsuspecting users. Many of my listeners told me they had feelings similar to those I harbored for *Two Dots*. Their obsessions ranged from *Clash of Clans* to Snapchat to *Words with Friends*. One person said that she probably spent more time looking at tips for cleaning her house on Pinterest than actually cleaning her house. "During the *Angry Birds* craze, my phone broke and I lost all my progress. I was so crushed," Robert wrote. "It still bothers me." By the way, Robert isn't a kid but a fully grown man with a job, kids, and other adult responsibilities.

Bored and Brilliant participants mirrored Flurry Analytics findings in other ways, too: Our mobile "addicts" also used messaging and social apps most. But games, news, media and entertainment, and utilities and productivity apps all featured pretty high usage. What is it about these apps that sparks such compulsive behavior? Why can't we swipe up and out of these frivolous pastimes the second that nagging bad feeling surfaces? Why does time spent so often snowball into time wasted? We aren't weak-willed, and it's not just the all-too-human proclivity to choose the easy distraction over more taxing work. We have an enabler, and it's the business model.

The Business of Building Addiction

The digital economy has been in large part built by app designers who are very good at making things we want to keep using, over and over and over. Even if—*especially* if—we pay with something even more precious than money—our time and attention.

Digital designer Golden Krishna, who made the salient point earlier that only tech companies and drug dealers describe their customers as "users," set about analyzing this troubling trend in an online manifesto, *The Best Interface Is No Interface*, which quickly went viral and spawned a book. Krishna's thesis spoke deeply to many *Note to Self* listeners like Dale, who described frustration with tech that "constantly wants to get in my face." It seems like a devil's pact to Dale, who asked, "I need to hand over my eyeballs, my attention, my time, and in return I get the tools to live my life?" According to Krishna, basically, yes.

Having worked for innovation labs at Samsung and Zappos, Krishna witnessed firsthand this shift in priorities from the historic definition of design as "solving people's core problems in an elegant way" to adding other features that "intentionally get you hooked."

So how did the tech industry get here? Is Silicon Valley filled with nefarious types who want to make us mindless so they can control our every move? Nah. Krishna breaks it down (elegantly) in his book and puts the blame on big data. "One of the really unfortunate parts about all this data is that organizations can get analytics-crazy," he writes. "Clicks are more easily measured than joy."

Facebook, Google, and all the big players use data dashboards that count things like how many times an app is opened or how much time the average user spends there as a way to assess their projects. Because they use those metrics to define success, companies naturally direct their resources to bolstering usage "rather than happiness or the real value to the end consumer." We respond to the ever-increasing notifications on our digital devices made by designers and developers under pressure to continue innovating those interruptions. It becomes a vicious cycle.

"What's unfortunate is the new media that's replaced old media uses the same business model, so as much as we talk about disruption or changing the economy, we're still using the same notion of selling ads for eyeballs," Krishna told me. Google, an investor in the home smart-device company Nest, has a large research and development division, and Facebook bought the virtual reality headset–maker Oculus VR. The big tech companies have plans to diversify how they make money. But for now, Krishna said, "those companies are largely getting their profit off of your time."

"Until these big businesses figure out new ways of revenue," he said, "we're going to be stuck in this mode of thinking."

Tristan Harris—who sold his start-up Apture, a service that enabled bloggers and media companies like *The Washington Post*, *The New York Times*, and *The Economist* to incorporate multimedia into their pages—agrees with the assessment that the current prevalent digital business model is a game to get people's attention. Or, as Harris put it, "a race to the bottom of the brain stem to seduce people's psychological instincts."

Having worked as a Google Design Ethicist and Product Philosopher until 2016, Harris has put a lot of thought into how technology takes advantage of our social inclinations and affects our behavior. He compares what's happening in the technological ecosphere to the growth of the food industry, which has made billions off our preference for salt, sugar, and fat. "Those are three ingredients that we really need and we're built to appreciate because they used to be really rare," he said. "Now there's a mismatch between our instincts, which tell us that those things are really good, and an environment that has abused them."

Basically, Harris is comparing our apps to a S'mores Frappuccino: sixteen ounces of cool, creamy sweet flavor containing nearly five hundred calories, with twenty grams of fat and sixty-seven grams of sugar that could have kept our ancestors trotting across the savanna for at least two weeks. Just as we are programmed to crave sugar and fat, no matter the cost to our wallets or waistlines, so do we desire novel information. Staying up to date can help us survive, whether it's staying away from a new pride of lions that's moved onto the plain or observing how your boss responds to public criticism on Twitter. "That's a useful bias to have," he said. "The problem is that in the attention economy, every player—meaning every service, every app, every Web site—is trying to figure out the best, most frequent way to tap into that bias." Now it's not outrunning a large beast that makes us feel alive, but rather collecting hearts on Instagram.

The most obvious examples of technological triggers are the settings and general design of text messaging apps and IMs. "When we message someone, by default we interrupt them, whether they are focusing on something or not," Harris said. "There's only one way to get a message, and that's to get the message right now."

Immediacy is a simple fact of modern life. Texts, in some form, are here to stay. However, these constant intrusions on our attention have serious costs, according to research by Gloria Mark, a professor of informatics at the University of California, Irvine. "About ten years ago, we found that people shifted their attention between online and offline activities about every three minutes on average," she said. "But now we're looking at more recent data, and we're finding that people are shifting every forty-five seconds when they work online."

This isn't just a productivity or focus issue. Mark's lab has found that the more people switch their attention, the higher their stress level. That is especially concerning, she says, because the modern workplace feeds on interruptions. Dubbing the group of workers most affected "information workers," she said this population "might have every intention of doing monochronic (concentrated) work, but if their boss sends them an e-mail or they feel social pressure to keep up with their e-mails, they have to keep responding to their e-mails and being interrupted." What could help?

"I think that if people were given the ability to signal to colleagues or just even to signal online, 'Hey, I'm working on this task, don't bother me, I'll let you know when I'm ready to be interrupted,'" she said.

But you can't blame your coworkers or your children or your Gchat buddy for everything. Guess who is the person who actually interrupts you the most? *Yourself.* Mark's lab has a term for this—the "pattern of self-interruption."

"From an observer's perspective, you're watching a person [and] they're typing in a Word document. And then, for no apparent reason, they suddenly stop what they're doing and they shift and look at e-mail or check Facebook. These kinds of self-interruptions happen almost as frequently as people are interrupted from external sources," Mark said. "So we find that when external interruptions are pretty high in any particular hour, then even if the level of external interruptions wanes [in the next hour], then people self-interrupt."

In other words, if you've had a hectic morning dealing with lots of e-mail and people stopping by your desk, you are more likely to start interrupting yourself. Interruptions are self-perpetuating.

Harris characterizes the current state of affairs that Mark describes as a "new kind of pollution, an inner pollution." Even someone like Harris, who thinks about this issue all the time, isn't immune to digital seductions. Before our conversation, he admitted he'd checked his e-mail and news feed "twenty times." No brain stem is immune.

But the source of Harris's true fear that we are losing the ability for reflection, restraint, and concentration comes from his personal experience running a start-up in Silicon Valley. "I'd walk into an office of an online publisher and say, 'We can double or triple the amount of time people spend on your Web site,'" he told me. "It's a moral conundrum that I faced as a founder and why I care a lot about this issue." The essence of the conundrum for any fledgling tech entrepreneur is that your ability to raise capital is based on proving you can exponentially grow usage.

As part of his desire to change "how we measure success," Harris began working on what he calls "design ethics," conversations and practices that can return some control over our technology to the "user" and, in turn, increase the value of the time we do spend with our devices. As part of this movement, which he calls Time Well Spent, he holds small designer meet-ups to share best practices, new forms of incentives, and products that "measure success in their net positive contribution to people's lives."

Is that even a real metric? According to Harris, it is. In 2007, Couchsurfing, a precursor site to Airbnb, where people could find places to stay for free all over the world, measured success in the "net positive hours that were created between two people's lives." The site used data such as how much time the couchsurfer and the host spent together and how positive the experience was (i.e., "Did you have a good time together?"). By Couchsurfing's calculus, the time two people initially spent searching profiles, sending messages, and setting up a stay on the Web site was factored as a negative, because "they didn't view that as a contribution to people's lives." That time was therefore subtracted from the original gains. "What you're left with is net positive hours that wouldn't exist if Couchsurfing didn't exist."

In the age of Tinder—the behemoth dating app whose success in 2016 is measured to the tune of 1.4 billion swipes a day rather than soul mates—I'm not optimistic.

Despite becoming so absorbed in our apps that we've lost sight of their original purpose, we should mobilize (pun intended), not despair, according to Harris, who views tech's evolution as parallel to so many other industries—including food's cheap, empty calories and banking's predatory lending. "I hate to say this, but if you surrender to the default settings of the world, they are designed to take advantage of you," he said. "Everything requires vigilance."

To take back our minds from apps like *Pokémon Go*, Harris advocates a political stance akin to what happened in the organic food movement, when consumers, angry over the unintended, detrimental effects of mass agricultural production, demanded new standards. We should imagine a world where success is aligned with the fulfillment of the user's original goals. Did you relax, feel connected to faraway friends, discover a new way to decorate your kitchen? The metric by which sites and apps should be rewarded, Harris argues, should revolve around the answer to this question: "Whatever people were looking for, did they get it?"

That sounds great. So do debt-free college, zero-waste homes, and a lot of other enormous societal visions, which are enormously difficult to make a reality. In the immediate term, Harris says, "The most important thing to acknowledge is that it's an unfair fight. On one side is a human being who's just trying to get on with her prefrontal cortex, which is a million years old and in charge of regulating attention. That's up against a thousand engineers on the other side of the screen, whose daily job is to break that and keep you scrolling on the infinite feed."

Belly of the Beast—a Q&A with the Creator of *Two Dots*

David Hohusen may not be evil. (Actually, he's a really nice guy.) But he *is* one of the geniuses behind *Two Dots*, the game that diabolically kept me connecting virtual bouncing balls rather than reading literature, cooking healthy meals, or just getting a good night's sleep. A year after its creation in 2014, the game reported close to five billion games played and fifteen million dollars in revenue. Ranked number eighty-six in Apple app store's all-time top-grossing games, *Two Dots* only continues to succeed and grow—thanks to addicts like me. Here's what the creator has to say about his game's "985 addictingly fun levels."

MANOUSH ZOMORODI: I'm actually very mad at you, because you're the person behind the dots that are driving me bonkers! What was going on in your brain when you made this game?

DAVID HOHUSEN: How do you create life with just a circle, or the feeling of life or a character with just a line? This is the stuff that I find super powerful. *Two Dots* was my first time working in a puzzle genre. I thought, *I need to make something that's really hard for me. If it's really challenging for me, and I can beat it, then other people will be able to beat it.* Unfortunately, after spending several hundred hours making a lot of levels, I got a little too good at the game. So some of the levels that I found extremely challenging were next to impossible for other players.

MZ: I'm doomed, because *Two Dots* seems to fit into all these little cracks in my life.

DH: That's the sort of game we're trying to make. In the game design itself, you have five lives—every time you lose a game, you lose a life. Once those five lives are up, you have to wait twenty minutes to get the game back, or you can pay. We don't make that much money from lives. It was designed to force people to not binge. We knew it would create this feeling of cheesecake that fits into that nook of your day. You can't have it all the time, which makes you want it more. If you ate all the cheese-cake, you wouldn't want it ever again. And that's what putting limits on these games creates in your brain; a feeling of it being more special than it actually is.

MZ: But by filling up all the cracks in my day with *Two Dots*, I feel like I'm handing all my creativity and daydreaming time to you.

DH: It's up to individuals to be smart enough about it. If you turn it into a reflex, you are stealing something pretty powerful from yourself. For me as a creative and as a game maker, I want to spend about half my time filling my little moments, my coffee-line moments, with playing games like *Two Dots*—having a really enjoyable experience waiting in line for a coffee and not just being annoyed that I'm in line. And I want the other half of the time to be a little bit bored so I can think of the next game I want to make.

MZ: Will you concede that in order for your business to thrive, some sort of a behavior manipulation has to happen that makes us need to return to these games over and over?

DH: Most people think of addiction as a negative. But in the mobile game space, they show it off. They tout it. The business side is concerned with how we can continue to climb the revenue chart on iTunes. To them, addiction is a very good thing because they want to see that number go up and up and up. They want to see ses-sions per day go up; they want to see duration go up. So do we as game designers, but we're incredibly mindful of the sort of tactics we use because we know if we make a game that's a little too underhanded, we're not going to feel great. Did we really make a great game or did we just use the dirtiest strategies to trick people into playing—which a lot of people are doing, not just with games. Tons of apps are doing it; Web sites are doing it. I like to think that users are smart enough that when they realize they've been tricked into a game with too many push notifications or other sleazy tactics, they will delete it. The thing is, no matter what you are making, if you're not careful, someone is going to release a similar app or game that has less of that stuff, and consumers are beginning to understand that.

MZ: Is the conversation beginning to change at all? Are there any people in the industry talking about whether digital media can be quantified by anything other than our eyeballs?

DH: I don't think they are. Not seriously. Right now, everybody basically wants to be Instagram. You want to get a billion users and sell your company to Facebook for all the money in the world. For a lot of tech start-ups, this is the driving motivation. Not ten thousand people using your app in a very meaningful way.

MZ: What are some of the tactics you don't like to see in games?

DH: A personal pet peeve is when people build games where you're basically rewarded for constantly checking in. They want you to open that app anywhere five-plus times a day. So every few hours, you're going in to check on something, and it becomes behavioral. Addictive repetition. It gets to the point where if you open your phone for anything—checking the weather, trying to figure out how to get to 16 Varick Street, opening a work e-mail—you're going to click on that game and tap something to get some sort of reward. Usually it's virtual currency, like virtual pumpkins in the game *Farm Heroes* or whatever.

MZ: Which sounds so stupid when you say it. Like, who cares about a virtual pumpkin? But it becomes very meaningful in some odd way.

DH: I think part of the reason that games are so intrinsic to our nature as human beings, why they've existed for so long and permeated throughout the generations, is because games are a measurement of success.

MZ: Well, if obsession is a measure of success, I'd say *Two Dots* has achieved it.

DH: The numbers are mind-boggling. In the last seven days, a hundred million games were played, and out of those hundred million games, a third of them took place on level 35. [Level 35, the last underwater level, is one of the first levels that Hohusen designed.] Some of these people have played this level a hundred times, and they still are stuck. That's when you're like, "Oh my god, what have we done?"

Can Video Games Be Good for Our Brains?

When I missed my subway stop the other day because I was so engrossed in *Two Dots* and therefore had fifteen fewer minutes with my children before bedtime, I tried to convince myself that the game was helping me decompress after work and potentially improve my spatial reasoning.

Hohusen believes playing digital games does have real-world benefits. "Committed game players—people like me, who have been playing games similar to the way athletes play sports—have the ability to make nonlinear decisions or to think five or six steps ahead." He doesn't see much of a difference between making progress in *Dark Souls* and "perfecting your serve in tennis or writing that piece of music that conveys an emotion."

According to a 2015 Pew report, about half of American adults "play video games on a computer, TV, game console, or portable device like a cell phone." That's a lot of people playing games. And we're not sure how we feel about it. "Public attitudes toward games—and the people who play them—are complex and often uncertain," the report stated. The truth is, we don't know whether games like *Two Dots* are good or bad for you (or simply a waste of time), because that question isn't easy to answer.

Of course, there are so many different kinds of games out there, from first-person and third-person shooter games to role-playing to strategy to brain games. But it's not as simple as CogniFit Brain Fitness = good, and *Grand Theft Auto* = bad. Researchers Dr. C. Shawn Green, at the University of Wisconsin–Madison, and Dr. Aaron R. Seitz, at the University of California, Riverside, found in a 2015 study that "action video games have been linked to improving attention skills, brain processing, and cognitive functions." But the games must have "quickly moving targets that come in and out of view, include large amounts of clutter, and . . . require the user to make rapid, accurate decisions."

Unfortunately, *Two Dots* doesn't make the cut. Neither do brain games, which the researchers said "typically embody few of the qualities of the commercial video games linked with cognitive improvement." In fact, in 2016, Lumos Labs, the company behind the popular brain-training app Lumosity, agreed to pay two million dollars to settle charges of deceptive advertising brought by the Federal Trade Commission. "Lumosity preyed on consumers' fears about age-related cognitive decline, suggesting their games could stave off memory loss, dementia, and even Alzheimer's disease," said Jessica Rich, director of the FTC's Bureau of Consumer Protection. "But Lumosity simply did not have the science to back up its ads."

The ineffectiveness of mobile games to improve brain functioning is something Dr. Zach Hambrick has been arguing for years. A professor of cognitive psychology at Michigan State University who studies learning, practice, and what it takes to get really good at something, he has tested the correlation between cognitive abilities such as problem solving and mobile games, "and we have yet to find evidence." Hambrick, who admits he isn't a "video game person," has written op-eds on this topic and was one of seventy neuroscientists who signed a letter of critique against the "brain-training industry."

"If you play *Ms. Pac-Man* a lot, you'll get better at Mr. *Pac-Man*," Hambrick summed it up, "and video games where you have to move through a maze. But you won't get better at some real task like filling out your tax forms or even *Space Invaders*."

So video games might not make us smarter, or better at doing our taxes, but can they help players cope with depression and anxiety? Jane McGonigal, director of game research and development at the Institute for the Future in Palo Alto, says they can do that and much more.

McGonigal was pursuing her PhD when she first became interested in studying the collective imagination and intelligence that can emerge when over a billion people spend about an hour a day playing video games. She went on to make many video games, including *Jane the Concussion-Slayer*, which she first built to help herself recover from a debilitating concussion. The game grew to a much wider audience as players started adapting the original for anything from dealing with bad breakups to losing weight to finding a new job. What began as a simple set of rules and goals (including daily quests, connecting with allies, collecting special powers, and battling bad guys) morphed into an app used by almost a million people that works to help them build resilience in the face of real-life issues. McGonigal renamed her game *SuperBetter* and also turned it into a book. "We're used to thinking about games as being the silly things," said McGonigal, "but maybe, maybe our fears and our self-hating sentiments are the silly things that we should be dismissive of."

To that end, she cited the renowned psychologist and specialist in play, Brian Sutton-Smith, who said the opposite of play isn't work; it's depression. Defining the essence of a game as "an unnecessary obstacle" where the goals you are trying to achieve are harder than they need to be (think golf, where players try to get a ball into a tiny hole on a huge course using a stick), McGonigal explains that games allow us to improve at something (anything!), and, by doing so, we experience excitement, physical energy, and pride in accomplishments. Combine those feelings with optimism, a sense of common ground, and shared attention, and people often discover games make reaching out to their fellow players far easier than connecting with others in everyday life. "Reverse all of those things," McGonigal said. "Having a hard time relating to others, lacking physical energy, feeling pessimistic about our abilities to succeed: that's literally the clinical definition of depression."

More recently, science has come to support what we intuitively know about the benefits of play. According to fMRI research, depression and video game play, in particular, are also opposites at a neurological level. The same two regions of the brain that are chronically understimulated when we're depressed are chronically hyperstimulated when we play video games. "To me, that is one of the most important things to understand right now, because it explains why many people self-medicate depression and anxiety with video games. It can also help us understand ways to use games more effectively so that they're not avoiding reality but provide that extra boost of motivation and optimism in reality."

So why have so many scientific studies come out against video games if brain scans show they can make us feel better? Just like studies on the effects of coffee and alcohol, news reports are pro one day and con the next. No wonder Americans don't know how they feel about them. Mc-Gonigal found the same conflicting information while researching her book *SuperBetter*, which included a meta-analysis of almost *five hundred* peer-reviewed studies on how game play affects real-life wellness (physical, emotional, social, professional, and academic). Half of them found that video games led to depression, social isolation, poor grades, and drug use, while the other half found the exact opposite, linking frequent video game play to greater happiness, stronger relationships, less drug use, better grades in school, and so on. "They're all great peer-reviewed studies in scientific publications," McGonigal said. "For many game researchers and designers over the past decade, the puzzling paradox is how to make sense of this divergent body of research."

McGonigal's big theory is that the "number-one indicator" of whether video games make a person's life and mood better, or have a negative impact on them, is if the player "sees games as being meaningfully related to reality."

"Are you a different person when you play? Are you in a different reality?" she asked. If so, "then you tend to use them as a crutch and aren't able to bridge the gap between a game world and your real-life challenges. So the worse real life gets, the more you play games, and then the more you play games, the more you avoid your problems in this downward spiral," McGonigal said. "The challenge is to enjoy or identify with the actions in the game, so that when you stop playing, you continue to love and enjoy them."

The idea is to play video games for "short bursts" in order to elevate one's mood and level of physical energy and then get "back to your everyday life in a more positive state." McGonigal encourages people to set a timer while they play video games. Playing for specific increments of time limits overplaying and avoidance of real life and has also been linked to different effects on the brain. For example, to be Zen with your game play, set your timer to twenty minutes. "A lot of video games have been shown to have very similar effects to meditation in terms of how the brain state is transformed," she said. "So if you're trying to calm your mind and body, and return to the world with more mindfulness, twenty minutes of game play time is recommended." Looking to squash cravings, stop an anxiety attack, or remove unhelpful, ruminating thoughts? Set your timer to ten minutes. "If you're trying not to overeat, smoke, or consume a drug, studies have found that ten minutes of certain types of games are really effective for that," McGonigal said. In order to keep the practice healthy and not fall into negative escapism, she explained, "You have to know the doses of game play the same way that you know to take two ibuprofen and not two hundred."

Self-regulation is not only key to accessing the benefits of video games, it is also another form of positive reinforcement. As with any practice, from meditating to keeping a journal to jogging, sticking to a personal commitment, no matter how small, can be a big confidence booster.

If we have to get tough about setting time limits, another important way to use video games healthfully is not to berate ourselves for the time we decide to spend playing them. "It's okay to use these games to purposely allow ourselves to not ruminate on anxious or depressive thoughts," McGonigal said, offering the example of the increasingly popular use of handheld games for children and adults before they undergo a surgical procedure to alleviate anxiety. "If they reduce suffering and allow us to stay committed to the actions that we want or need to take, games shouldn't be considered a negative distraction but rather really effective," McGonigal said. "If there's been one gift to humanity from the world of video games and video game research, it has been that we now better understand a lot of ways that we can alter our brain state nonpharmaceutically. This is a tool that's affordable and doesn't have side effects."

Well, the only side effect is if you *can't* regulate your video game usage through a timer or whatever means, and it turns into an addiction that only exacerbates all the problems it was meant to solve in the first place. McGonigal, however, bristles against this popular notion of addiction. "Addiction science is going through an incredible radical reinvention right now," she said. "What's changing in the field is the disease model of addiction—the notion that addictive substances, such as cocaine or alcohol, do something to our brain that change it irreparably for the worse.

So looking at other things, such as social media, cell phones, and video games, through that same rubric, because they activate the same regions of the brain, is a mistake."

The new prevailing theory, according to McGonigal, is that addiction is not about a "broken brain." When someone has an addiction, his or her brain is working similarly to a "healthy" brain, in that both are motivated to achieve pleasure and positive outcomes. The only problem with an "addicted" brain is that it's fallen into a rut of seeking those pleasures from only one particular, often detrimental, stimulus. "For some people, that stimulus is a physical substance like a drug; for some, it's a person they're falling in love with. It's whatever gets fixated on in the reward loop of the brain," McGonigal said. "Some people do get that loop fixated on video games, or social media likes." Following this logic, to combat addiction, offer the brain alternative sources of satisfaction. "What you need to do is expand your brain's awareness of other things that activate it in the same way," said McGonigal, who encourages players to think and talk about video games within the broader concepts of life off-screen. Don't think how good you've gotten at shooting robots, consider how well you've learned to concentrate and focus for short periods of time.

So when I complained that I might have an addictive personality when it came to *Two Dots* at least, McGonigal told me "there's no such thing." Instead, she argued for "addictive circumstances," situations in which I ought to seek pleasure from other places. While I would easily stop connecting squares if someone were calling for help or I had to do a radio interview, if I'm simply facing a pile of dirty dinner dishes—not so much. "Let's not infantilize ourselves by saying we can't," she said. "You keep playing because you prefer that state to whatever the alternative is."

McGonigal doesn't just talk games; she plays them, too. Now on level 894, she's been playing *Candy Crush* for about five minutes every day for several years. "I like that game a lot," she said. Although it goes against the science that says blue light from the phone interferes with sleep, bedtime is exactly when she likes to indulge in a little *CC*. "I use the game to turn off," said the mom of eighteen-month-old twins. After her children go to sleep, around 7:30 P.M., she returns immediately to work until it's time for her to go to bed. "I have to switch my brain from superproductive planning, slightly anxious mode to not having thoughts in my head about what I have to do." *Candy Crush* provides the perfect transition. "It's one of those flow-inducing games that allows you to focus on nothing other than the game," she said. "A level or two of that, and my brain is effectively switched away from things that might otherwise have me lying awake, planning." Sleep tight, Jane.

One person's incredible waste of time is another's wonderful tool for improving mood and mind. "What I recommend that individuals who feel addicted to games do," McGonigal offered, "is focus on what is the abstract quality of these games they really love, so they can find it in other things."

Hambrick had very different advice for anyone with a video game problem.

"Contact your therapist," he said.

When I brought up this debate with *Two Dots* creator David Hohusen, I was surprised to learn that he'd also given up certain games because they'd become a problem for him. "Oh, yeah," he said. "I do it all the time." He cited *World of Warcraft*, the massive multiplayer online role-playing game so addictive, there is a Wowaholics Anonymous group to "help those negatively affected by *World of Warcraft* addiction." He played it while the game was still being tested in beta, but never again once it launched, Hohusen explained, "because I knew that if I did, it would take over my life."

Make Your Own Warning Label

Meet David Joerg. Although he's a dad of two little girls, he's the one with a curfew (though his is set by an algorithm, not a parent). See, David has a problem with video games. Especially at night.

The poison of choice for this software developer is *StarCraft* (created by the same company responsible for *World of Warcraft*). David's story might sound familiar by now. After putting the kids to bed, he loved to unwind with his favorite game and "sometimes I get a tub of Nutella, some crackers, maybe a bottle of port. Maybe one of the three, or maybe all of them. And then it's time to party!"

Sounds fun, but as the night sped by and his wife went to sleep hours before he did, *StarCraft* turned more into a compulsion than a pastime. By 1:30 A.M., David was looking at the clock, thinking, *This is ridiculous*. But all too often, if he hadn't won a game yet, he couldn't bear to go to sleep without winning just one. So 1:30 A.M. turned into 2 A.M. in the blink of an eye, and by this point, he knew he was going to be exhausted anyway, so he might as well play again. Finally at 3 A.M., David put the game down and went to sleep for a whopping three and a half hours before he had to get up at 6:30 A.M. "There are some people who only need that much sleep, and I am not one of them," he said. "I would be destroyed the next day and limping through like a zombie."

If this were a once-in-a-while Nutella, port, and *StarCraft* all-night-long party, that would be one thing, but David's binges went on for a few years, despite the fact that he made many attempts to give them up. Forget about setting a timer. "I tried a calendar reminder, with an appointment to go to bed every night at 10 P.M.," he said. "I tried to have rules for myself and wrote down my excuses when I broke them so I could see how lamé they were. I tried to write what I wanted to accomplish the next day and establish a bedtime routine. I got a sleep tracker." They all worked—for about two weeks, and then David would relapse.

Finally, when he was about to crack from lack of sleep, David turned to the software developer within to create "a system that would beat me." Here's what he did:

- He linked his sleep tracker to his computer and set it to *keep him out* after curfew time at 10 P.M.
- Once curfew time hits, his computer browsers—including his video games—shut down until 6 A.M. the following morning.
- He denied himself administrator access to his computer, because, he says, "If I had the root password, I could just override the system."
- Instead, he saved a new, ridiculously long password on five pieces of paper and put them in places difficult to get to late at night, including across town at the office, shoved inside his daughter's piggybank, and in the

drawer of his wife's nightstand. "She's a pretty light
sleeper, so if I try to sneak over to the nightstand to get it,
she's going to jump up and slap me on the wrist. And
that'll be game over."

David's goal was to get, on average, seven and a half hours of sleep
every night, and with his elaborate system, he's been achieving it. But—
wow—when you see how much one man has to go through to resist
sleep deprivation from a video game, it's more than a little scary.

"I know enough about habit-forming and even addictive technology
that I don't touch this stuff," said Nir Eyal, a digital marketing expert
and the author of *Hooked: How to Build Habit-Forming Products*, about
the kind of behavior engineering that makes apps and games so hard to
put down. "I used to be in the gaming and advertising industries. Let's
face it, these industries are based on mind control."

Eyal's not talking about subliminal messages sent through the patterns of dots but documented psychological theories built into products
such as the endowed progress effect. That phenomenon describes what
happens in the mind when we get close to achieving a goal. Wanting
mastery and completion, the brain is more likely to pursue finishing
something that it thinks is close to completion. The progress bar on
LinkedIn that shows you are just a few steps away from a perfectly complete profile and getting just one more cat in *Neko Atsume* are just two
examples of how designers encourage people to stay on an app, Web
site, or game.

This kind of manipulation is a basic rule of life in the digital era,
but Eyal argues it's time for companies to at least acknowledge their
tactics—particularly since, unlike in eras past, creators of addictive
products are now in a position to help those they hurt. "Let's face it, this
is nothing new; addiction has been around for a long time," he said.
"But if you were an alcohol distiller, you could throw up your hands and
say, 'It's not our problem. How do we know who is abusing our product?'
Today these companies know. *Two Dots*, *Candy Crush*, Facebook, and
Twitter all know exactly how much you're using their products.

"Maybe," Eyal said, "it's the upside of collecting all this data about us."

Differentiating between addiction and habit formation (defining the former as something that "hurts a user who can't stop" versus negative behavior that can be altered simply by moderating use), Eyal says the vast majority of people fall into the second camp: "What generally happens is, there's a craze—we're into *Flappy Bird* or *Farmville* or *Two Dots*. Then when we figure out this is not making my life any better, most of us will delete those apps." There is a small percentage who can't handle technology, just like those who can't handle liquor or food. He estimates this group to be between 2 and 5 percent of all users, and while that number might seem small, Eyal still advocates for a "use and abuse" policy that labels digital products as potentially addictive.

You don't need to be an expert to know we are a long way from the day when *Two Dots* comes with a SMOKING KILLS–style warning label. Until then, the only thing we can do is create our own warning label by asking ourselves this simple yet fundamental question, offered by Eyal, every time we download, upgrade, or power up anything digital: "Is this product serving me or hurting me?"

Getting Kids to Put Down the Console

One of the statistics Sherry Turkle quotes in her book *Reclaiming Conversation* is that over 40 percent of teenagers never unplug—not when they're at dinner, doing homework, during a religious service, or even when they go to sleep. Teens have always stayed up late, but the average adolescent should get two more hours of sleep a night than she actually does. There are, of course, a number of reasons for that. (The public argument has been made that high school should start later in the morning because teenagers' natural internal clock keeps them up late.) But a major factor contributing to lack of sleep these days is the smartphone.

Eighteen-year-old Temitayo Fagbenle, one of the extremely talented young reporters in WNYC's Radio Rookies program, gave a telling first-person description of how technology disrupts kids' sleep: "I'll wake up in the middle of the night, around 3 A.M., and I'll just see Instagram or Facebook and be, like, 'Double tap if you're up.' Or, 'Like my status if you're up. Who wants to talk?'"

This is the subject of a lot of my listeners' letters to the show. They want to know if and how they can limit their children's digital time, consumed mostly by video games, social media, and apps. (Chapter 7 goes into more depth on technology and parenting.) When it comes to mobile games specifically, if Americans in general are ambivalent about them, no subset is more so than parents. Should they let their children play video games? If so, which ones and for how long?

Just as with adults, games expert and champion McGonigal believes that for kids, it isn't so much about which game but how you play it. To steer children into becoming players who don't use games to escape real life but instead become more confident, focused, social, and creative problem solvers, there is one thing no parent should ever do. "Do not shame your children about the games they play," she said.

That means never saying things such as "Stop wasting your time and do something real." Trivializing a kid's favorite video game will not get him or her to stop playing. It will only serve to "develop that escapist mind-set" by reinforcing the idea that their interests don't matter and that games don't have a connection with the real world. Instead, engage with children by asking questions about the game. How you play it. What's hard. What's cool. How they've gotten better at the game. You know, the basics. They'll probably roll their eyes at you, but McGonigal said, "That conversation alone can really transform a young person in terms of their ability to bring all of these gameful strengths to school, to sports, to their personal relationships, and to themselves." In fact, one listener reached out to me on Twitter to tell me that he knew a mother and father who heard my discussion with McGonigal and had reached out to their now college-aged son to apologize for berating his video game habits. It was a "healing" moment, the listener wrote. Especially important now that this son has decided to major in computer science.

As to what games McGonigal recommends for kids, she said, "Any game that requires you to study it to understand its rules, opportunities, and resources. Any game that is genuinely challenging." Does that include shoot-'em-ups like *Call of Duty*? McGonigal conceded that she doesn't personally play games in which you have to "kill creatures" and so doesn't encourage others to play them either. "But for people who are drawn to those games, there is quite a lot of evidence that when you play them with people you know in real life—whether on a team or online with friends in their homes playing—there are many cognitive, social, and emotional benefits."

The key, however, is to play with *real* people whom you know and with whom you have a real connection—even if they are across the country. As McGonigal explained, "We don't see those benefits in the first-person shooter world when you are mostly playing against people you don't know in the anonymous Internet game play." That's because there is a negative effect associated with playing violent games when the opponent is anonymous. "This is the same thing that leads to flame wars on the Internet and a lot of vicious trolling," she explained. "When you don't know the other person, you don't have any social consequences for beating or defeating them, being a poor sport when you win." This can also lead to players' becoming increasingly aggressive and less kind to those they perceive as weaker.

McGonigal calls this phenomenon "testosterone poisoning," a terrifying concept. But she has a simple and direct prescription for the malady. "If you love these games, you need to spend at least half of your time or more playing with people you know."

With all games, she recommends helping children make the connection between what they do on-screen and real life by—*sigh*—quizzing them. Yes, add this to your modern parenting repertoire. She counsels parents to ask their kids what they have gotten better at since they began playing a game. However, the important aspect to this question is to get at the abstract skills. So if your daughter answers, "I got better at slinging this bird," or your son says, "I'm really good at using this kind of power-up," you have to dig deeper. Push them to move past the concrete tasks and get into the larger skills behind them—such as "I found trying different strategies helps with this level." I tried this with my son after his first slumber party. He was thrilled that I wanted to talk video games and responded with enthusiasm when I asked him what it took to be good at the game he and his buddies played. "You really had to think hard and focus!"

"If they can talk about these abstract things, then what happens through the game play is they're building up a positive identity that they can experiment with," McGonigal said. "But those are skills and resources and abilities that persist in their mind outside of the game world, which you as a parent have a really important role in cultivating."

CHALLENGE FOUR: Delete That App

When I thought about Nir Eyal's question, "Is this product serving me or hurting me?" I knew I had to delete *Two Dots*. I *wanted* to delete it. And yet the process was literally nauseating. First I had to check what level I was on (perfectly illustrating the investment phase of the hook model of games, which comes after the trigger, action, and reward steps). Then I had to mourn the loss of that level. I'd worked hard to get into the triple digits!

I pressed down on my apps, watched them all jiggle, moved my thumb over to the *Two Dots* icon, and, with a moment or two of hesitation, hit the small X. And like that, the thing that had filled all those little cracks in my day was gone. I then needed some alone time to process my loss.

But if I can do it, so can you.

Your instructions for today: Delete it. Delete *that* app. I'm not just talking about games but social media, too. (I know for some of you, the idea of deleting Facebook or Twitter is almost a fate worse than death. I promise, you'll live.) It could be anything—a weather app or even Wikipedia. You know which one is your albatross. The one you use too much. The one you use to escape—too often, at the expense of other things (including sleep). The one that makes you feel bad about yourself. Delete said time-wasting, bad-habit app. Uninstall it.

CHALLENGE UPGRADE

If you want to kick your kicking-the-habit up a notch, don't just delete the app from your phone—delete your whole account. I had people tell me they took Facebook and Twitter off their phone for the campaign, but after the presidential election, they went whole hog and deleted their account. No one is saying you have to do this. But if you find your life is way better without these apps, you might want to consider it. Remember, you are in control.

This was by far the hardest challenge for the original *Note to Self* listeners who followed the Bored and Brilliant program—myself included. As Sandra, a college student, put it, "This task was just cruel."

The app she decided to delete was Instagram, because, she said, "I check that app much more often than I actually need to, and I'm not even sure why." Sandra is far from alone in having a mindless Instagram problem. After deleting it, however, she realized that her habit of scrolling had brought a level of comfort. "I felt a bit lost for a while," she admitted. Looking for another use for her phone, Sandra decided to call people. *Gasp*. She phoned a few friends with whom she wound up playing Frisbee in the park, which she called "a much better use of my time."

Sandra, who was able to regulate her Instagram use after putting the app back on her phone once Bored and Brilliant week was over, is more mature than I am. I have to keep *Two Dots* off my phone. But after completing this challenge, other Bored and Brilliant participants say they now do weekly or monthly fasts from certain apps. Like Aaron, who struggled to delete Twitter, then figured out that he didn't have to give it up forever. "I could just stop using it for a day. It ended up being a lot easier than I thought, so I've decided to go ahead and do it every week," he said about his No-Twitter Mondays.

Try the challenge and see where you land on the app-abstinence spectrum.

Notes on Challenge Four

"I did it, with great pain. I deleted all the time-suck games on my phone (and resisted the urge to check out *Two Dots* after listening to the podcast). I also deleted FaceSuck and PinHorder. It's good for me, I know it is, I don't plan on installing them again, but *whoa*, that was way more difficult than I had thought it was going to be."

—Nat

"I'm embarrassed by this one. It's a dumb game—*AE Bubble*—that I get sucked into while I'm watching movies, while I'm waiting for friends, etc. But my husband is thrilled. Seriously thrilled that it's off my phone. So, thank you. I guess."

—Ellen

"After reading these comments and seeing people actually deleting Facebook, which I am *not* doing, I decided to delete not only *Two Dots* and Feedly, but also my main game addiction: killer sudoku. It's gone! No more 'I'll just keep going a few more minutes until I get stuck.' I feel liberated."

—Jane

"After a brief period of really a horrible withdrawal feeling from no Twitter, like a lack-of-caffeine head-ache, I now feel great and had a lovely dinner with my family."

—Cathy

"I deleted Facebook, which should also help with taking photos and posting them. It feels like I cut off my index finger! *Ugh!* The madness!"

—Randolph

6

Doing the Deep Work

*For creating the time ... Freedom©, \ Self
Control©*

> *—Zadie Smith's acknowledgments to two
> Internet-blocking programs for her novel* NW

Back in 2004, when BlackBerries were still called CrackBerries, the Boston Consulting Group agreed to a risky experiment.

To set the scene, BCG, as it's known, is a global management consulting firm of twelve thousand employees who bring in five billion dollars in revenue from the biggest companies around the world. Typically, BCG consultants were always on call, ready to respond to a wealthy client's request for strategic advice or data analysis, no matter what time zone. "They needed to have that BlackBerry on their nightstand, and when it buzzed, they'd wake up," said Matthew Krentz, a senior partner.

This is exactly what mobile technology was made to do—create a workforce on demand 24/7 for maximum productivity, right?

Wrong.

Krentz and his fellow BCG upper-management colleagues discovered that perpetual connectivity was good in the short term—not so much in the long term. Simply put, these consultants were totally cracked out.

"What we found was that while we attracted people with great talent who were excited to join BCG, we were also losing them three, four, five years later, when they found the life unsustainable," Krentz said. The company had a serious retention problem.

So Krentz and his colleagues agreed to let researchers at Harvard Business School turn them into time-management guinea pigs. Professor Leslie Perlow asked a small team of BCG consultants to do something radical: take *time off* in the middle of the week—no work, no e-mail, no cell phone. In fact, the suggestion was to "do something relaxing."

Rather than react with relief, the consultants panicked. The BCG culture was to check e-mail religiously, cancel plans with family and friends whenever necessary, or, in reality, skip making plans outside work entirely. Perlow assured them that one team member would always be kept on standby for calls, and none of them would be penalized by the clients or the company.

So, they gave it a try.

Each consultant picked a day when he had to turn off completely and refrain from checking e-mail or responding in any way to a fellow team member or the project leader. Instead, he or she was to exercise, cook, or just hang out at home with family and friends.

And here's what happened:

Not only did the consultants reclaim their personal lives, but back at the office, team members started talking to each other more. As a result of covering for each other during offline periods, they started communicating more, keeping each other in the loop through conversation, both one-on-one and as a group. The added benefit from the experiment was more big-picture ideas. Some unplugging resulted in less time wasted sweating the small stuff, like stressing over typed-up meeting notes or perfecting the latest round of pie chart slides. They got better at planning and prioritizing and reported brainstorming more solutions, too.

Results were so good that more than a decade later, the program, which goes by PTO for "predictability, teaming, and open communications," is still used by thousands of teams in almost all of BCG's seventy-eight offices around the world. "These facilitated teams report a seventy-five percent higher likelihood they will stay at BCG for the long term," Krentz said. Instead of paying top-level consultants big money to stay constantly connected, they pay them to avoid burnout and regularly disconnect. BCG has spent eleven years on *Fortune*'s "100 Best Companies to Work For" (including six years in a row as one of the top five).

The promise of technology in the workplace is precisely to increase efficiency and productivity. But anyone who has been on an interminable e-mail chain knows that the digital realm can be a tremendous time-suck. Many of the tools that allow us to work wherever and whenever we want also condition us to work with divided attention. Whether it's a conversation over Gchat or the constant notification of new e-mails in our in-box, we have come to accept, even expect, frequent interruptions. And every time we respond to a ping or bubble, it takes *twenty-three minutes and fifteen seconds*, on average, to get back to what we were originally working on, according to Gloria Mark's research! No wonder it often feels like a miracle when we complete any project or report at all.

The real casualty of all this distraction is the "deep work." In his book *Deep Work: Rules for Focused Success in a Distracted World*, Cal Newport of Georgetown University's computer science department defines the term as "the ability to focus without distraction on a cognitively demanding task." He writes that this ability, which allows for mastery of complicated information, is "one of the most valuable skills in our economy" while at the same time becoming "increasingly rare."

Malia Mason, a cognitive psychologist and associate professor of management at Columbia Business School who studies how competing motives shape our judgments and choices, argues that while technology's microintrusions are partly to blame for our waning ability to concentrate, the blurred line between work and life, thanks to our mobile devices, is the real culprit. It might seem like a boon to employers to have their workforce always connected and "thinking about work outside the office." But the downside is that "while employees are at work, they're thinking about their social lives or home."

"When I sit down to work on a project or a work problem," Mason said, "I'm suddenly thinking about the carrots I need to get for my son Bobby's lunch. Our lives are too integrated now."

Wow—work–life integration was the whole point of a lot of technological advances. But if we want to do anything more interesting and important than just answering e-mails and IMs, it seems a separation is necessary. "The problem is not technology, it's with how we're using it," Mason said. "We're at a place where technology is consuming our limited mindshare instead of giving us the mental space to have brilliant thoughts."

A *Note to Self* listener described the phenomenon perfectly when she wrote, "I often find myself on my phone to answer an e-mail or a text for work, and then I get distracted by Facebook or Instagram or whatever. I'll put my phone down only to realize that I never did what I turned to my phone for in the first place."

Deep thinking and the creativity that it nurtures are hampered by the way we use technology to satisfy superficial notions of productivity (think deleting e-mail). This worries the MacArthur Genius Grant–winning host of *Radiolab*, Jad Abumrad, who credits his parents for forcing him to practice music daily as a child. Alone, in a small room with only a piano for company, he says he was conditioned to focus, which later gave him the foundation for achieving success as an adult.

"Any show that I make is really stupidly tedious for most of the process," Abumrad said. That's really surprising, considering his radio show and podcast, which spans science, philosophy, and the human condition, covers big, exciting topics like "How did we go from tiny bags of chemicals to the vast menagerie of creatures we see around us?" And poses mind-bending questions like "Is it possible to understand everything?" or could we live in "a world without words"?

But, yes, even exploring such heady subjects has its dull side. Abumrad describes transcribing hours of interviews and dozens of revisions on the final product. (It took me a year, culminating in an all-nighter, to complete the *Radiolab* episode I did with Jad.) "It doesn't feel creative at all," Abumrad said. "It's almost like organizing thumbtacks. It's not that fun." The ability to be bored is so crucial to Abumrad that when he described the young people who succeed at *Radiolab*, he said they're "people who just have a tolerance for that tedium. That's it."

The Instant-Gratification Economy

Forming new habits isn't just about ending your Instagram or *Two Dots* habit. As *New York Times* reporter and Pulitzer Prize winner Charles Duhigg described in his book *The Power of Habit*, which spent over sixty weeks on his paper's best-seller lists, many companies use technology to recalibrate our demands as consumers and then fulfill them. *Now.* Selling instant gratification is nothing new (hello, McDonald's), but the time span for the fulfillment of the product is getting shorter and shorter. Amazon used to have free shipping for its Prime members. Now it's free *same-day* shipping.

Duhigg says Uber, the car service app, is a great example of a company using technology to make the consumer feel like it's delivering a service faster and better. "In cities like New York, hailing a cab isn't necessarily harder than ordering an Uber," he said. "But what Uber does is it sets up your expectations precisely right, so that when the car comes, it's incredibly gratifying." Anyone who has used the app knows just how reassuring it is to see that little car moving closer and closer to the pickup location.

Not much is fundamentally different about what, say, Uber or Seamless, the food-delivery site, offers. The novelty is a new kind of certainty. Neither app requires you to pull out your credit card at the end of the ride or tip the delivery person. You know exactly when your car or food will arrive, and there's no need to speak to a human being on the phone. "Studies show when there is any kind of ambiguity in any type of setting, it causes a certain amount of stress," he said. "So when a company can say to you, this is exactly how it's going to work, that feels very comforting and rewarding." It might also be the reason why so many of us avoid talking on the phone at all costs now.

Online requests can't be misinterpreted; we can track and know the reward is coming as quickly as possible. But are these services truly the most efficient? In 2013, journalist Alexis Madrigal wrote a piece in *The Atlantic* describing the flow we get lulled into by technologies that encourage us to keep scrolling rather than actually achieve anything. NYU anthropologist Natasha Dow Schüll, who spent a decade in Las Vegas studying slot machines, labeled that hypnotized feeling certain sites give us as "the machine zone."

Slot machines, historically loss leaders for casinos and kept around only to occupy the wives of high rollers, have an interesting relationship to the digital era. According to Duhigg, the entire business was overhauled when the largest company in the industry hired someone from Sega video games to remake their machines. That included creating different levels of rewards that are simultaneously expected *and* unexpected, subliminal *and* overt, intermittent *and* consistent. Sure, players still won money or points, but they also got showered with bright lights and noises. In observing people play these new types of slot machines, Schüll discovered that all time and space fell away with the lights and pings—and that winning money was no longer solely the point for players. They got in the machine zone, and, as a result, as Madrigal noted in his piece, slots have "exploded in profitability during the digital era as game designers have optimized them to keep people playing."

At a structural level, pushing buttons on a slot machine on the casino floor isn't that different from scrolling through Pinterest for children's birthday cakes or Houzz for kitchen lighting fixtures. "The websites that are succeeding right now know this, and they design themselves explicitly to try and deliver to you something rewarding," Duhigg said, although these rewards, unlike services such as Uber, aren't tangible. So you might find the perfect cake or copper pendant, but you'll also enjoy some eye (and brain) candy.

New Workplace Expectations

While all the tools in our offices have grown as stimulating and diverting as slot machines, workplace values have gone the other way. An IBM survey of fifteen hundred CEOs from more than thirty-three industries across sixty countries found that the single most important quality in "successfully navigating an increasingly complex world" is *creativity.*

What's particularly interesting is that this survey of establishment business leaders was released in 2010, on the heels of the worst economic crisis of these executives' careers and with a wave of new platforms and social networks propelling every industry into the Information Age.

You might think that in such unstable and unpredictable times, they would prize "rigor, management discipline, integrity or even vision" over creativity. But faced with more data and competition piled on top of financial pressures, business leaders agreed they must change strategy more quickly, nimbly restructure staff and resources, sometimes even re-think their core product. Longevity now requires the ability to pivot and innovate—and the best chance for that is creativity. No wonder it was voted, according to IBM's senior VP, "the number one leadership com-petency of the successful enterprise of the future."

Yet is the digital environment—the very thing enabling greater knowl-edge and connectivity around the globe—actually stunting our capacity to thrive in it?

Andy Haldane, the Bank of England's chief economist, seems to think so. "We are clearly in the midst of an information revolution, with close to ninety-nine percent of the entire stock of information ever created having been generated this century," he said. "This has had real benefits. But it may also have had cognitive costs. One of those potential costs is shorter attention spans."

Of course, Haldane is more worried about the financial implications than Britons' ability to get through Shakespeare. In a speech he deliv-ered in 2015 at the University of East Anglia, the chief economist talked about far-reaching trends created by our loss of sustained concentration—including in the area of finance. "Average holding periods of assets have fallen tenfold since 1950," he said. "The rising incidence of attention deficit disorders, and the rising prominence of Twitter, may be further evidence of shortening attention spans."

That's putting a lot of the responsibility on the shoulders of Twitter. Even if Haldane's singling out of the social networking service seems harsh, it makes his larger point that technology encourages "the fast-thinking, reflexive, impatient part of the brain to expand its influence." That in turn minimizes the kind of slow foundation building and per-sistence crucial to long-term economic growth. To further prove his point, Haldane pointed to the fact that spending by UK companies on research and development has been on the decline for a decade.

If you agree that the current state of affairs is hampering our ability to do the deep work—whether that's growing a Fortune 500 company or writing a poem—the question then becomes, how does one find the space to think in the digital era?

Artists have always understood that solitude—boredom, even—is essential to the creative process. Now economists, social policy experts, and scientists are making the argument that it's vital for business, too. The Imagination Institute's Scott Barry Kaufman and science writer Carolyn Gregoire brought the case for mind-wandering and other forms of reflection to the *Harvard Business Review* in an essay with the pretty direct title of "Executives, Protect Your Alone Time."

Although tailored to the work world, their rationale should be a pretty familiar one by now. We live in times that are not conducive to solitary reflection, which "feeds the creative mind." You know—how it's crucial for our brains not to respond to tasks or immediate stimuli or even concentrate on a singular topic but to sometimes just space out, mind-wander. Contrary to what your boss may think, it's not being lazy. This is when the brain's default mode network kicks in and our best, more original ideas get gestating, because we dip into profound and hidden reservoirs of emotion, memory, and thought. Many areas of the brain are lit up as we bring together past, present, and future to imagine entirely new realms and ways to do things (oh, and new products).

But you need alone or quiet time, and when we carry our offices in our pockets, that becomes all but impossible. It's almost a badge of honor to always be checking e-mail, as if the more you have to refresh your inbox, the more important you must be. Or if you don't respond to a group e-mail or message, you're not a team player. (Stay-at-home parents suffer equally from this phenomenon: think of those stupid class e-mail threads where parents reply-all with "Great!" or "Thanks!" or "We can't make it but have fun!") But neuroscientists say that if we are always responding, we don't take time to think up new ideas. "Today's culture overemphasizes the importance of constant social interaction, due in part to social media," Kaufman and Gregoire write. "We tend to view time spent alone as time wasted or as an indication of an antisocial or melancholy personality. Instead, we should see it as a sign of emotional maturity and healthy psychological development."

Most workplaces these days don't exactly encourage quiet reflection, but they should if they want to get the most out of their employees. Kaufman and Gregoire offered some tips for managers to help their teams "reclaim solitude and improve their ability to think creatively—without diminishing collaboration."

Some of their ideas include giving people more freedom to work off-site, especially when they are assigned projects that require creativity. Who doesn't get more work done at home or at a café when they really need to concentrate? Still, Kaufman and Gregoire suggest that managers put aside a room designated for quiet work only. Their biggest recommendation, however, is more a change of mind-set than architectural configuration. Those in charge should value and promote employees' occasional need for seclusion, even if it just means taking a walk outside for a bit (without checking the phone).

There is one surefire way to unplug from the office, and that's taking a vacation. A real one, where you don't work. Unfortunately, Americans have a terrible habit of not using all the vacation days they are entitled to in their jobs. A 2016 survey conducted by NPR, the Robert Wood Johnson Foundation, and the Harvard T.H. Chan School of Public Health found that about half those in the United States who work fifty-plus hours a week reported that they don't take all or even most of the vacation they've earned. Thirty percent of those who do get away "do a significant amount of work while on vacation."

That is bad business for your brain. "Managers should . . . urge employees to take all their vacation days," Kaufman and Gregoire write in the *Harvard Business Review*. "Having time for periodic rest and reflection will give your team the space to replenish their creative energy."

Bored and Brilliant Business—European Edition

Europeans have a tradition of taking time off very seriously. In 2016, when French president François Hollande and his cabinet pushed to get rid of the country's thirty-five-hour workweek, more than thirty thousand people took to the streets of Paris in protest. There's nothing about that sentence that makes sense in an American context. The United States has the unique distinction of being the only developed country without any legally required paid vacation days for workers. Meanwhile, every country in the European Union has at least four workweeks of paid vacation by law.

New incursions into personal time posed by technology haven't lessened the European resolve to relax. Germany has been at the forefront of the mission to curb digital creep with a combination of government regulation and private sector initiatives. In 2012, Volkswagen made the bold move of shutting down its BlackBerry servers so that they stop routing e-mails thirty minutes after the end of employee shifts. The servers start cranking again thirty minutes before their shifts begin. The effort (which does not apply to senior management) was explicitly put into place to draw a line between work and home.

A growing number of German companies have since followed suit—including Deutsche Telekom, the energy giant E.ON, and Henkel, which produces home, beauty, and adhesive products. Each business, however, has taken a unique approach to the problem. The automotive company Daimler allows employees to automatically delete any e-mails that come into their in-box while they are on vacation. BMW created a system that has employees and supervisors come ·up with a mutually agreed-upon amount of work they will do away from the office—for which they are reimbursed.

The German government also launched its own efforts to protect workers' mental health and improve productivity by drawing a clear line between when they need to be available and when they don't. Starting in 2013, the German labor ministry banned its managers from contacting staff after regular hours—by phone or e-mail—unless it is an emergency. The code called for managers to practice "minimum intervention" when breaking into workers' personal time and to make sure the number of people involved in any intrusion is as few as possible.

The French government wanted to take similar legislation and apply it not just to government workers but all of its citizens with a 2016 amendment that would grant the "right to disconnect." Part of a broader bill to reform many labor laws in France, "The Adaptation of Work Rights to the Digital Era" makes it illegal for companies of fifty or more employees to send e-mails to employees outside regular work hours. Au revoir, stomach-churning, weekend-ruining message from the boss on Friday night or idiotic reply-alls that disrupt perfectly good crossword time on Sunday morning.

Quiet Time

Unless you plan on moving to Germany or France, where they have legislation on work e-mails coming in after hours, the onus is on you to take charge of when and how to disconnect from the never-ending flow of information.

That's part of what Susan Cain, author of the bestselling *Quiet: The Power of Introverts in a World That Can't Stop Talking*, is trying to do with her latest project, Quiet Revolution. From parenting quiet children to finding career success as a quiet person, Cain is working to build solitude into the culture of our schools and our workplaces. On the corporate side, she has created the Quiet Leadership Institute, a management consulting firm that advises clients such as General Electric, Procter & Gamble, and NASA on how to harness the talents of introverts.

"The idea is that a third to a half of the population is introverted," Cain said. "That's at least one out of every three people. Yet we live in a society that is telling everyone to be an extrovert. What that leads to is a colossal waste of energy and talent and ultimately happiness."

The advent of social media and total connectivity has only made this cultural bias toward extroversion more pronounced. The truth is, many of us—whether we're introverts, extroverts, or ambiverts—feel drained by our devices. The big question, though, is how to extricate yourself from incessant digital interactions, especially if you have your own business or have a career that requires an active social media presence. How can those who feel fatigued and overwhelmed balance our desire for quiet with a need to keep up with everyone else?

Considering the dilemma of giving oneself crucial restorative breaks and finding the discipline to enforce them, no matter how enticing the app or intense the pressure from the work environment to respond in real time, Cain suggests that the first hurdle is cultural: "not seeing the need for quiet contemplation as a weakness but as part of being your most productive self."

On the whole, our society doesn't prioritize or value solitude. My experience with teenagers is that they are not comfortable spending (or encouraged to spend) much time alone. If they're not at school or with friends, they're on Snapchat. And their parents aren't much better. I often hear people always say they could never go to a restaurant, movie, or vacation by themselves. It's as if alone time is scary.

"Oh yes," Cain agrees. "From the time children are two years old, they are sent explicit and implicit messages that it's not okay to play by yourself. You should be playing with others. There is something *wrong* with solitude."

Happiness and success at all ages are conflated with being popular, outgoing, confident in a strong-handshake-and-forceful-voice kind of way. Social, Cain believes, is defined in a "narrow and oppressive way." A third of the population absolutely requires periods of seclusion to be most effective at their jobs, but, according to Cain, all of us need time alone to do good work.

So, she says, reject the idea that wanting to be alone is a sign of weakness. "We've got to get rid of it completely!" Cain said. "Solitude is one of our great superpowers, and it always has been." For her book, she interviewed some of the toughest introverts around, including General Stanley McChrystal—who led the U.S. military's secretive Joint Special Operations Command through the Gulf wars for the longest stretch in the command's history as well as all U.S. and NATO forces in Afghanistan—and U.S. Marine Commandant General Charles Krulak, the highest-ranking officer in the United States Marine Corps and a member of the Joint Chiefs of Staff. Both men told her that solitude is the key to making effective decisions as well as building the courage and conviction to stand by those decisions.

The steely-eyed general who needs alone time to think through life-and-death decisions is one thing. But in most contemporary places of work, the quiet person can often be dubbed weird or egocentric. That's especially true in the recent cult of collaboration arising out of such partnerships as Google's Larry Page and Sergey Brin and Apple's Steve Wozniak and Steve Jobs. "There have been so many amazing creations and inventions that have come from 'collaboration' that there's now a mythic status around the very word," Cain said.

The current craze in corporate America, which loves the latest trends in ingenuity, is insisting that only a group of people can spark an exchange of the best ideas. According to a 2014 innovation report conducted by Nielsen, "Two in three consumer product professionals rank collaboration among the top three most critical factors for innovation success, outpacing strong leadership and access to financial resources."

Cain isn't buying the idea that groupthink is "where the magic happens." "For a lot of creative people, being in a group is like kryptonite," she said.

In his memoir, *iWoz: Computer Geek to Cult Icon: How I Invented the Personal Computer, Co-Founded Apple, and Had Fun Doing It*, Steve Wozniak backs up Cain's theory on the critical place of intellectual solitude in the creative process. In no uncertain terms. "Most inventors and engineers I've met are like me—they're shy and they live in their heads," he writes:

> They're almost like artists. In fact, the very best of them are artists. And artists work best alone—best outside of corporate environments, best where they can control an invention's design without a lot of other people designing it for marketing or some other committee. I don't believe anything really revolutionary has ever been invented by committee. . . . I'm going to give you some advice that might be hard to take. That advice is: Work alone. . . . Not on a committee. Not on a team.

The Tech Industry's Famous Introverts

Guy Kawasaki: One of the Apple employees originally responsible for marketing Macintosh computers, he calls himself a "secular evangelist" and doesn't sound like a shy guy. Still, the Silicon Valley venture capitalist is a self-proclaimed introvert.

Facebook founder Mark Zuckerberg: At least that's what Facebook COO Sheryl Sandberg says.

Google founder Larry Page: You won't see this guy wearing a headset while offering motivational messages about the future to packed auditoriums anytime soon. He avoids giving keynote talks at conferences or press interviews like they are the plague. So far it isn't hurting business.

Yahoo CEO Marissa Mayer: Well, she has posed lounging on a lawn chair for *Vogue* but says she gets extreme social anxiety at events, even when she's the host. In terms of prizing solitude for her employees, she stirred up a lot of anger when she banned working from home, which was a popular practice at Yahoo. She defended her decision by saying that while "people are more productive when they're alone," they are "more collaborative and innovative when they're together." That sounds nice, but the decision might have had more to do with the fact that when she checked up on how many times people working from home logged into the company's network, she discovered quitting time came around too early.

Bill Gates: The Microsoft founder himself put it best when he said, "Introverts can do quite well. If you're clever, you can learn to get the benefits of being an introvert, which might be, say, being willing to go off for a few days and think about a tough problem, read everything you can, push yourself very hard to think out on the edge of that area." (While Gates ran Microsoft, he famously took "Think Weeks," when he would go into seclusion twice a year for one week.)

It's hard to develop a new idea if you don't even know what it is yet. In our world of instantaneous reactions and decision making, the best concepts still usually need time to germinate before they grow into actual plans. Cain advises business leaders to send people away, even in the middle of a meeting, to give them time to incubate their ideas by jotting down notes or whatever solitary process suits them.

Amazon founder and CEO Jeff Bezos begins most of his staff meetings with thirty minutes of silent time during which staff are supposed to quietly read a carefully prepared six-page memo geared toward the meeting. He prefers these mission-driven memos to bullet-point slide presentations because he believes full sentences and paragraphs force "a deeper clarity." That clarity comes on two levels—one is the presenter, who can offer more nuanced issues and complex thoughts through prose, and two involves the participants, who get time to focus and digest the material.

Cain hopes that companies and the people who run them don't view solitude as just another behavioral trend, like mindfulness or open-office plans. "From a business point of view, this has to do with embracing a results-oriented workplace where everybody is focused on whether we are delivering good work or not," she said. "How much you're sitting at your desk is irrelevant. All that matters are the results, and you end up getting the best results when people feel the freedom to get away and put their head down and work for four hours without being interrupted; or if they have a door to their office, that it's socially acceptable to close the door without being seen as unfriendly."

To truly take control of our bored time in a business setting, we can't feel guilty about it. While action—or inaction, as it were—might look lazy or strange to others—if the results are top-quality work, nobody should shame you. So the responsibility lies within us and not our bosses—or our smartphones. "Until recently, we have tended to think that the solutions for tech overload must be technological in nature," Cain said. "But really, the solutions are emotional and psychological. At their core, they have to do with self-awareness."

Hmmm. Sounds a lot like mindfulness. Or maybe we should call it "personal observation." In any case, it sounds hard, like adding a step to our already jam-packed to-do lists. But it's achievable, according to Cain, if you follow the general rules for success in any new discipline or endeavor: Create targeted goals and experiment with strategies to get you there until you land on the methods that work best for you. "A lot of it is negotiating an agreement with yourself," she said. "Basically, setting boundaries and not having too much fear of missing out on the stuff that you're not going to do."

So that might mean interacting with your Facebook followers for a set amount of time every day—say, one hour—and then pulling the plug. Or maybe it's attending a set number of networking events. Only you know which activities drain you most. And, of course, you have to hold yourself to your agreement . . . with yourself. While Cain advises setting limits on the amount of time you are connected or interacting with others, "you have to equally assign yourself the unplugging and restorative time." Choosing a time frame is the most important step to making it happen. (In other words, show yourself how serious you are by blocking out time in your calendar to walk around your office's industrial park at 3:30 P.M.) The other important factor is scheduling "restorative breaks in small chunks all throughout the day." These can be as small as getting up for a glass of water and stretching, or scheduling a ten-minute call to a friend. Cain advised against what one *Note to Self* listener described as his schedule of working like crazy all week and then completely going dark over the weekends. "That sounds really nice," she said, "but I would hate to come back on Monday morning and have to answer the hundreds of e-mails piled up in the meantime."

My Silent Workspace

When I thought more clearly about the "deepest" work I do, it became very clear that writing—whether it's the weekly podcast script, a talk, an op-ed, or this book—carries the most weight. A quick e-mail response or post on Twitter gets washed away pretty quickly, but something I've given original thought to can travel and take on a life of its own. And frankly, it might make a difference in someone's life. But I knew I was getting none of this "deep work" done at the office or at home, surrounded by chatty colleagues (radio people *love* to talk) or kitchen counters just begging to be wiped down. I needed discipline and quiet. So I joined a silent workspace. Now, "silent workspace" is my terminology. I had tried "co-working" or shared workspaces before, but I couldn't concentrate with other people yakking on the phone or "collaborating." But then I discovered the Brooklyn Writers Space, which has a no-talking, no-phone, no-noise policy. Walk up the stairs, and there's a small kitchen area where you can crunch and chew your lunch to your heart's content. But step past the next door and into the sanctuary of work carrels, and the only sound you make should be typing. No snacks allowed (too much potential for smacking lips or crinkling wrappers). If you get a call, better make sure you leave as quickly and quietly as possible to take it . . . and don't start talking until you've reached the outside hallway. (You can talk there or on the sidewalk downstairs. Neither has heat.) I'd always thought a place like this was for novelists, people who were writing masterpieces that would take readers to other worlds full of narrative neuroses and passionate intellectual escapism. But now I realize we all have quiet work to do. Just because your job isn't to literally write a story, that doesn't mean you don't need the headspace to take a mental journey and craft whatever it is you make—whether it's a spreadsheet, corporate report, or computer code—to the deepest and best of your ability. Give me four hours of my quiet workspace just twice a month, and you'll see better output than all the rest of my time at the office combined. The price of admission ends up paying for itself.

CHALLENGE FIVE: Take a Fakecation

Entrepreneurs, executives, employees, and anyone else whose job involves creative problem solving needs some solitude in order to focus and really think up some new and interesting ideas. It's during those breaks from e-mail, texting, social media, and calls that interrupt all day long when connections are made and insights refined. But, as Cain prescribed, you need to assign yourself the necessary unplugging by seeing that restorative time not as a weakness but as the key to your most productive self.

Get ready to take a fakecation. A vacation in the form of a break from the digital onslaught that exhausts, distracts, and keeps us from thinking beyond the everyday.

This challenge is one of my favorites. It gives me breathing room—relief from the pressure to read and respond. It's a chance to finish a thought and stop feeling like a goldfish. But I think the best part is knowing that you've recalibrated the sender's expectations. The first time I was on the receiving end of an away message (from my manager, actually), I laughed out loud and felt so happy for her . . . and glad to wait until she was back in e-mail-responding mode. I knew she was making the best use of her time and that my question (about an upcoming event) wasn't urgent. The tension of an unanswered e-mail dissolved.

Decide how long you need: An afternoon? An hour? Twenty minutes? It's up to you. If there's no way your boss will let you be off the grid for an hour or twenty minutes, set aside time for yourself tonight. The important thing is to set a fixed period (I suggest looking at your calendar the day before and choosing the least demanding time to unplug) and to stick to it! Also, don't feel the need to be honest. You can say you have an urgent doctor's appointment or family emergency, if you are dealing with an unreasonable human on the other side. But save this card for when you really need to play it. Also, don't think, *Oh, it's just an hour. I'll manage without the bother of setting up an outgoing message.* Yes, but will you fully relax and stop checking your e-mail and so forth during that hour? Give yourself the permission of time that's accounted for, both in your mind and the recipient's.

To ease the stress of this fakecation (and poke fun at the crazy time-management situations these platforms have put us in), I recommend crafting a tongue-in-cheek away message, like "More face time, less Facebook. Give me a call if you absolutely need me." Post your away message on e-mail or Twitter, Facebook, GroupMe, Snapchat, or Instagram—anywhere people normally reach you. If you don't exactly know how to let people know you're taking a break, feel free to use one of the suggestions below:

> "Hello! I'm focusing in on a project right now, but I'm planning to check all my e-mails at 4 P.M. today. If it's urgent, contact me with a real, old-fashioned phone call."

"Preparing the next generation to take over the world! I'm on a digital hiatus to spend a little more time with my family."

"Consciously uncoupling from my phone for the day."

"Teched out, checked out. Taking a little break from the devices. Thanks for your patience."

CHALLENGE UPGRADE

Upgrade your vacation to include taking a hiatus from not just e-mails and phone calls (although, let's be honest, who really gets calls anymore?) but also text messages. Consider an app that sends automatic responses to incoming texts just like an outgoing message on your phone or e-mail. Good ones to use are anti–texting and driving apps, such as AT&T DriveMode (it's available for iPhone and Android regardless of your carrier) and OneTap. Both hide or silence incoming texts and send out auto-reply messages.

Notes on Challenge Five

"Yesterday I unplugged completely from lunchtime onward (I work from home) and so enjoyed the peace of it that I kept going all the way until bedtime. I read *paper* papers, hung out with a friend, and got some quality sleep. I'm more determined than ever to reclaim my analog time, space, energy, attention, and *life*—while recalibrating my relationship to the digital world around me."

—Sally

"I have been pretty darn good at keeping up with your challenges, Manoush, but today just couldn't do it. So I'd like to counterpropose that I take a Sabbath from all things e-mail, Twitter, etc., on Friday night and Saturday. It's one way of observing Shabbat that lends some true quality time to my life. I will turn the lights on and off, I won't check e-mail. So here's my away message: 'Hi and thanks for your message. When the sun set on Friday, I checked outta e-mail land and tuned into friends and fam. But not to worry. Once the sun sets on Saturday, I'll put this message back in its box and reach out to you. Now put your phone down and go play.'"

—Talia

"This is what I posted on Facebook: I am participating in the Bored and Brilliant challenge. I will not be on public media for the next day or so, but still love you."

—Anna

"I signed off Twitter and Facebook this morning, and as I was walking to work I had the most fantastic idea. It may have been a coincidence but I'm giving the credit to B & B!"

—Peter

"I am by no means involved in a tech-related job, so this challenge should be easy for me, right? Wrong. I serve tables and bartend, which means that there can be short periods of nonproductivity. We are usually urged to polish glasses, or fold napkins, or some other brainless activity to give the customers the illusion that we are, indeed, productive individuals. What really happens is quick and consistent phone checking. 'Who's texted me?' or 'I have to tweet about this crazy allergy this lady has' or 'Hmmm, has Gaga posted on Instagram today?' Tonight when I work, I will go on a social media hiatus. I'm hoping to engage more with my coworkers, think of new ideas to improve my workplace, and maybe even meet someone interesting who would have previously been underprioritized due to Twitter."

—Maya

"I can't really detach from work e-mail, so I'll ignore personal e-mail and texting. Wish me luck! P.S. Day Two of no Facebook, and it feels good."

—Marie

7

Reclaiming Wonder

*Part of doing something is listening. We are
listening. To the sun. To the stars. To the wind.*
—*Madeleine L'Engle,* A Swiftly Tilting Planet

There were so many great stories, revelations, and insights from the first
Bored and Brilliant challenge I did with my listeners. But one of my
favorites came from Florida high school teacher Joel Adams, whose
class completed the weeklong program together. "I'm not sure if my students really comprehend how mediated their daily life really is, how
many images, and Snapchats and Vines and Instagrams they make and
send each day," he said about his motivation to engage his students in
our communal experiment.

After just a week of small changes to how they used their smartphones, Joel saw big results. There was a marked jump in class participa-
tion. (What teacher doesn't like that?) Adams also felt that by training
their attention on how they use their devices, his students became more
aware and savvier about how they work. But *my* favorite outcome was that
after the Bored and Brilliant week, there was more student eye contact—
between him and the kids, and among the kids themselves.

While the news from Mr. Adams's class made my heart sing, it also
hit upon the deepest, darkest anxieties any of us who are parents or
are related to or work with young people have. Many of us are concerned
about the ways in which technology is affecting the future of our children's

relationships, their ability to creatively engage in society, and the very quality of their existence. Jason, a *Note to Self* listener with two children, summed up how a lot of us feel when he wrote, "My greatest fear is that my kids will become shut-ins and not learn how to connect with people."

Well, Jason, Dr. Mary Helen Immordino-Yang's findings from a two-year study she did on the correlation between how adolescents use media and what that means for their ability to manage their lives confirm that you should listen to your parental intuition.

The neuroscientist and human development psychologist began tracking the media use of a group of Los Angeles downtown and inner-city kids at the ages of fourteen and fifteen years old. Immordino-Yang's tracking included their social multitasking—such as what kinds of social media the kids used and how many other ways they were interacting while they were doing things like their homework. Two years later, she and her team did a series of tasks with the group. The kids were asked to imagine solutions to world problems, react to real-life stories, and predict where they would be in their lives a year from now and ten years from now.

Although her findings are preliminary, Immordino-Yang reported a "very intriguing correlation that kids who were more engaged and multitasking with social media were actually less empathic in their reactions to other people. They also are less imaginative two years later about their own possible future and about solutions to world problems, like violence in their neighborhood for example."

Great. Just what every parent struggling to get their teen off Snapchat for a second wants to hear.

Of course, Immordino-Yang's findings make sense in the context of what we already discussed: how technology can inhibit the prospective thinking that comes with mind-wandering—the way we use our memories and understanding of present circumstances to figure out the best way to move forward. But the role of computers, smartphones, and tablets is only continuing to grow in the lives of children. That raises the question: how do tech gadgets and digital media fit into effective and caring parenting?

My stomach churns whenever I read something about how tech leaders don't let their own kids use the very gadgets and software they make. *The New York Times* reported in 2011 that the CTO of eBay, among other executives and engineers from Google, Yahoo, Apple, and Hewlett-Packard, sent their kids to the no-tech Waldorf school in Los Altos, California. Adhering to the educational philosophy that favors activities like cooking or knitting around wooden tables (using natural materials for everything from toys to furniture is a hallmark of its methodology), the Silicon Valley school doesn't believe in exposing children to computers before seventh grade, because it can "hamper their ability to fully develop strong bodies, healthy habits of discipline and self-control, fluency with creative and artistic expression and flexible and agile minds."

Even Steve Jobs, the father of the personal computer, put severe restrictions on his children's use of digital gadgets, according to Nick Bilton, author of several books, including the bestselling *Hatching Twitter*. Bilton wrote a piece for *The New York Times* with the self-explanatory title "Steve Jobs Was a Low-Tech Parent." In it, he reported that in 2010 when he asked Jobs, "Hey, how do your kids like the iPad?" the father of the iPad barked at him, "They don't. We limit tech in our house."

"I was completely shocked," said Bilton, who talked to other Silicon Valley big shots for his piece. *Wired*'s former editor-in-chief Chris Anderson, who now runs a drone-manufacturing company, is also very strict when it comes to the tech use of his five children. "There is absolutely no screen time during the week," Bilton said of Anderson's long list of rules, which included no gadgets allowed in the bedroom. Ever.

Bilton said that Jobs banned gadgets at the dinner table. "Dinnertime was devoted to talking about history and art and books and things like that."

Steve Jobs, the man who created the iPhone and iPad, restricted his children's use of them. This makes me think there's something he knew about his products that he never shared. Like a drug dealer who doesn't touch the stuff that he deals.

To be fair, I suspect it's a lot easier to force your kids to put down the iPad when you have staff and the kind of support system afforded to the rich and powerful, which might include a chef preparing your family a beautiful, organic, locally sourced meal. For the rest of us mere mortals—who have to live in a digitally oriented universe where sometimes, in order to make dinner, you need to park a toddler in front of YouTube—are dog videos going to be the newest way to wreck your kids?

Before you move to a yurt in some New Mexico desert, Joel Levin, a New York City father of two young children and cofounder of the independent game development company TeacherGaming, offers an optimistic and practical outlook on our children's future in a digital world. Part of Levin's positive outlook comes from his own experience. A member of the Atari 2600 generation, Levin learned how to program computers so he could make his own games. "I was always taking apart computers, much to my parents' dismay," he said. Later, as a computer teacher at a private school in New York City, he tried bringing games into his classroom, with varying degrees of success.

But then in 2011, he started playing *Minecraft* and almost immediately knew it had the makings of a great teaching tool. For the uninitiated, *Minecraft* has since become a national obsession for young people who love building and taking apart the digital blocks, which kind of look like Legos, to create their own virtual world. *Minecraft* is referred to as a "sandbox game," because the only goals are to explore, have fun, and *make*. "There's no winning in *Minecraft*," Joel said. "You create what you want or you connect with your friends and you go on adventures together, or you stand there and you kill zombies over and over and over. It's really what you as the player bring to the game."

In much the way the Institute for the Future's Jane McGonigal described how games can benefit a child's development, Levin watched his eldest daughter, who wasn't even five at the time, go through elaborate thought processes as she tried to figure out how to build and fix things in the *Minecraft* world. She also learned to spell her first word. Levin had set up the game so that if she got lost, he could type the word "home," and she'd find herself right back in her *Minecraft* house. One day she approached him and said, "Daddy, how do you spell 'home'?" Even more exciting to Levin—and his daughter—was her virtual construction of a tree house. "She was very proud to show me the tree house and all the little rooms and features she had made," he said. "Building a tree house is not an experience that she's likely to have as a girl growing up in New York City."

Seeing a world of possibility, Levin designed a two-week *Minecraft* unit for his second graders. "There was an explosion of joy in my classroom like I had never seen before," he said. "I would give them challenges and limited resources, and they would have to work out ways to accomplish their goals creatively. These seven-years-olds were really engaged with the material and open to the higher-end discussions about strategy and overcoming personal differences that I was hoping to get out of them."

It was such an incredible experience for Levin that he began spreading the word about *Minecraft*'s educational properties to anyone who'd listen. He started a blog about it, which gained the attention of reporters and other teachers who wanted to mimic his experiment. He was so zealous, he earned the nickname "*Minecraft* Teacher."

Levin eventually partnered with the Swedish creators of *Minecraft* to create an educational version of the game called *MinecraftEdu*, which is now used in upward of seven thousand classrooms across more than forty countries on pretty much every topic. There are prebuilt worlds like the Forbidden City of the Ming Dynasty or prehistoric ones, where students can excavate dinosaur fossils. There's a world called Decimal Island, where students can "spawn on an isolated island where they will quickly be tasked with finding the three hidden quests on the island. Each question will have to do with addition and subtraction of decimals." Santa Ana Unified School District uses educational *Minecraft* to have elementary school students rebuild the local historical sites they learn about in social studies. In Louisville, Kentucky, one school has created a *Minecraft* world based on the different Common Core standards.

There's no research yet to prove that *MinecraftEdu* improves academic results. (Academic improvement in general is a hard thing to prove, no matter the pedagogical tool. Still, in 2016, University of Maine researchers announced a two-million-dollar grant to study the game's effect on student interest in science, math, and engineering.) Testing scores aside, *MinecraftEdu* is indeed an appealing concept. It brings together all the best aspects of technology—the limitlessness of imagination, ease of experimentation, and teamwork building through human collaboration.

And yet, *MinecraftEdu* is just a small sliver of the technology that touches most children and adolescents. Whether it's depressive symptoms that go hand in hand with the constant social comparisons that Facebook facilitates (something actually found in a study by the University of Houston) or the manipulative design techniques employed by app developers, so much of the digital ecosystem's side effects don't seem all that great for anyone, let alone kids. Maybe that's why even Levin doesn't give his children *any* time in front of screens Monday through Thursday. "No screens at all, period," he said. "No debate."

MODELING GOOD DIGITAL BEHAVIOR

During the first Bored and Brilliant challenge week, I heard from quite a few parents who felt guilty about using their phones instead of playing with their kids or enjoying more meaningful personal time. On the whole, parents had more phone time than nonparents, but they picked up their phones less often.

Do you have children?	Average minutes per day	Average pickups per day
No	82	42
Yes	103	34
Prefer not to answer	97	29

The average age of parents in our survey subgroup was forty, whereas nonparents averaged around thirty years old. So our parents' phone stats might just have been a reflection of another trend—people seem to change the way they use their phones as they age. The older you are, the fewer pickups you have. But older people generally stay on their phone longer each time they unlock it. And remember, this isn't generally phone calls and talking—it's screen time.

Age range	Average minutes per day	Average pickups per day
14–19	104	66
20–29	87	65
30–39	94	52
40–49	96	34
50–59	83	39
60–69	81	27

You don't exactly have to be a child psychologist or pediatric neurologist to know that limiting the time children spend on devices is crucial. Content, however, is just as important an issue. And the content delivered by many apps, Web sites, and games can be harmful, according to Dr. Susan Linn, cofounder of the Campaign for a Commercial-Free Childhood.

Having worked with the hero of children's television, Fred Rogers, before becoming a psychologist, Linn is unequivocal about the unique threat she sees posed toward youth by today's media landscape. It really irks her when people—particularly those her age, who have already raised a family—dismiss parents' fears by saying, "My kids watched TV, and they're fine."

"No parents in history have ever had to cope with the unprecedented convergence of ubiquitous, sophisticated, alluring, habit-forming screen technology and unfettered, unregulated advertising," she said. "That combination is the major problem."

Although she retired from her post as director of the Campaign for a Commercial-Free Childhood, Linn's raison d'être is to take on big corporations and their marketers through her organization, which forced media giant Disney to give refunds on its Baby Einstein video series. "They were claiming they were educational for babies, and in fact they're not educational for babies," she said.

In 2014, Linn and CCFC also won a settlement against Facebook for, among other things, using the names and images of teenagers in ads without permission from their parents. Although the settlement of $290,000 was a pittance for Facebook, at the time, that sum represented 90 percent of Commercial-Free Childhood's entire annual budget. Yet Linn turned down the money in order to pursue further action against the company. "When we think about children using screen devices, the primary way they're targeted . . . we have to remember the business model is advertising and marketing," she said. "It's collecting private personal information to sell to advertisers or embedding product placement. It's just kind of endless."

Although she admits to being biased, Linn says *Mister Rogers' Neighborhood* was an interactive experience of a different sort. "The kids weren't swiping," she said, "but Fred was encouraging them to think and feel—and encouraging them to turn off the TV."

~~Letters~~ Texts from Camp

Digital devices are just another ingredient in the great soup of parenting, which at its essence is about giving children the tools to become capable, independent adults. Those tools include self-regulation and measured decision making. So while many of us Gen X and Millennial parents seem to struggle with this, parenting does require setting limits and loosening the tether. While we want to instill good habits in our kids at a young and malleable age, there is wisdom in also giving them freedom to make mistakes, experiment with boundaries, and find their own rhythms.

Enter Matt Smith, the director of Camp Longacre in rural Pennsylvania. I met Smith when I went to observe a radical experiment he conducted at the camp his family has been running for forty years.

Let me set the scene. On a woodsy hilltop dotted with tents, the two-hundred-acre farm where Camp Longacre is located has exactly the organic-farming-community-building-exhuberant-but-not-too-crazy-competitive spirit that would attract a lot of helicopter parents nervous about sending their offspring away for the summer. The campers, who refer to each other as "farmers," milk goats, collect eggs, pick fresh lettuce, and go on wholesome outings to nearby Hershey Park and the lo-cal bowling alley.

Longacre is exactly the perfect place to give kids a break from their gadgets. Who needs apps when you have friends to make, crushes to obsess over, and lanyards to braid?

But here's where the experiment comes in. Smith decided to make a shocking break from the way his camp and most camps do business when it comes to tech. Instead of making all campers hand over their phones and tablets for the duration of their camp experience, he established a new "anything goes" gadget policy.

"Anything goes" might be overstating the case a bit. There were always going to be times when devices were not allowed, such as activity periods. No iPhones while canoeing. Mostly, though, devices were to remain in students' possession—even at night.

The idea behind this seismic shift in camp policy came from Smith's belief that for teenagers today, leadership isn't about learning to take charge. It's about learning how to make decisions, take considered actions, and set boundaries. Our constant attachment to the digital sphere, however, poses an obstacle to kids developing those skills, according to Smith.

"This generation is the first to be grappling with this. They grew up with screens and smartphone technology," he said. "We just figured if we are going to prepare them for life, part of that preparation has to be learning to find balance in their lives with technology."

So rather than mandate a digital blackout, he decided to help his campers develop ways to cope with their devices.

Smith didn't come to this decision easily. It took a long time and a lot of debate within the Longacre community. But if the goal of Longacre is to "prepare kids for long-term success," then Smith and his family felt they were failing when it came to technology. He'd seen campers who couldn't imagine five minutes without texting or checking Twitter spend the summer detoxing only to "fall back into old habits and resume old tendencies with their technology" when they went home and back to school. Even those kids who could identify that they "didn't like the way their phones always made them feel . . . weren't adjusting their behavior."

"They just don't have the skills to manage the access to technology," he said.

Still, when I first talked to Smith in June, before camp and Longacre's new policy had started, he was nervous. Part of the apprehension was because of the reaction he got from devoted families. "Many of them were not happy with it," he said. He was even worried about what effect the new policy could have on his business. Although certain parents saw the potential upside to the new rules, for the most part, "people were very frustrated with us." A lot of their concern, Smith felt, stemmed from a romantic view of the past. Many parents, former campers themselves, worried iPhones and the like would destroy any chance of losing track of time among the mosquitoes and hormones that they so fondly remembered.

All Smith could say was that at Longacre, the emphasis is on "life skills" and that if they wanted the idyllic cell-free atmosphere of the past, then literally thousands of other programs out there offer it. When I asked him if he modeled his new policy after another camp, he said, "Certainly not. We couldn't find another residential program that did this." There were travel and academic camps that let the kids have gadgets but no other traditional summer camps. In fact, one of the biggest surprises, Smith said, was the reaction he received from other summer camp professionals to his "anything goes" policy, which he only described euphemistically as "strong."

So in true trailblazing style, Longacre welcomed the first group of campers with smartphones, tablets, and other digital devices for the summer of 2013.

On day one, campers were required to hand over their gadgets to Smith and stay tech-free—just for the first week—so they could get to know one another face-to-face.

Then the campers were reunited with their gadgets. And all hell broke loose.

Kids ran to the Octagon, the only cabin with electricity, to plug in. Relying on the spotty 3G access of rural Pennsylvania, they ignored each other and holed up in tent corners to tweet, update Facebook, text, call, and be gamified.

Kimmy, a girl from Long Island, described those first hours back with her phone as an out-of-body experience: "I know this sounds strange, but I didn't even know where I was. I was, like, wait—am I talking to my friends or am I at camp?"

In the time it took to power up, the "anything goes" experiment seemed like a disaster. Maybe instead of *anything*, it should have been macramé from 10 A.M. to 11 A.M. and iPhones from 11 A.M. to noon. But like all good camp directors, Smith did not stray from his plan. "The most important thing that we do at Longacre is model appropriate behavior," he said. That meant the counselors weren't on Facebook or Snapchat and used their phones for business purposes only. The second piece is education, said Smith, who made books on the topic of technology available to the campers and encouraged them to "discuss it with people [meaning him, the counselors, and some other campers] who are thinking a lot about it."

Education and good role models? I'll admit I was skeptical. But when I visited Longacre camp in late July, not only had the kids leveled out in their tech usage, some had even grown philosophical about it. During my stay, I saw a lot of hugging and handholding. There was kitchen duty, gardening, lasso instruction, swimming, lots of singing, and a cave-exploration field trip. Fun stuff. (Allowing devices also had the unforeseen benefit of seriously improving the quality of music at camp. Before "anything goes" was instituted, Smith said, "It was tough. We relied on the radio and told kids to bring CDs." But who has CDs anymore? "There was a summer song that was on the radio all the time, and it was terrible.")

Most important, though, many campers also decided to set tech limits for themselves . . . and for their friends.

Kids who wore their headphones too often got dirty looks. Some campers restricted themselves to texting during quiet time. One girl even handed her phone back to Smith. She felt the constant contact with her friends and family reignited the homesickness that had abated during her first week. Most of the teens, however, were able to strike a balance between milking goats and texting friends from their bunks.

On the whole, Smith says he thinks his campers were more at ease when their gadgets were tucked away. "Adolescents want to socialize, be accepted, try new behaviors, separate from their parents," he said. "Those are all normal behaviors, and I understand why social media can [have] an allure. But camp and other kids can provide that."

Smith may be biased, though, with his own wistful memories. Kids, raised on the stuff, have a different relationship to technology than their parents do. Gadgets are as fully integrated into the human experience as, well, other humans. As one teenage boy said, "People don't see technology as tools anymore. They see them as friends."

NOTES ON A DAY IN THE DIGITAL LIFE, BY AN ANONYMOUS THIRTEEN-YEAR-OLD
—In the morning I get ready, without my phone.
—Then I get on the bus and I play *Candy Crush*, listen to music, scroll through Instagram b/c it's boring on the bus.
—I watch YouTube videos. I go on Vine. When I go on Instagram, I check on mostly famous people and what they're posting.
—There were people making fun of me on Twitter, so I kind of deleted it. Mainly, the reason thirteen-year-olds use Twitter is because they like to stalk their celebrity crushes.
—I feel like sometimes I need to be off of my phone because I'm so bored.
—I think teens should have an hour on the phone and two hours without the phone. You should put away phones during homework.
—My school has a strict no-phones policy. But after school, with friends, they say, "Oh my god, look what this person posted?" And you're sort of obliged. Is that the word?

CHALLENGE SIX: Observe Something Else

"The wonder of childhood" is a common phrase, but what does it really mean? It's certainly not only, or even mostly, that picture of idyllic, long days spent skipping rope and frolicking in nature—as parents angry over Camp Longacre's new technology policy might have hoped.

Part of the reason children get so absorbed by technology is that they get absorbed by anything that is stimulating! When everything is new, of course there's wonder, an energetic fascination with the world, virtual or real, before the weight of experience and responsibility gets in the way.

I want to suggest that we adults reclaim a little offline wonder for ourselves. Not only will it be stimulating for us, but, as Smith suggested, the best way to teach children something is to model it for them. Why do we want our kids to pry themselves away from Facebook or *Minecraft* (no matter how educational)? Because we want them to pick up their little heads and look at all that's happening around them in any given time and place. But how can we model this behavior when our own faces are tipped down at screens? Well, friends, we are lifting our chins yet again today.

For our second-to-last challenge, you will train the attention we've been freeing up all week on what the futurist Rita King calls the "un-inventable details" of life. Now that you've begun limiting time spent swiping past strangers' selfies, baby pictures, and career updates, check out what's really going on around you—which, as many of those who did the first Bored and Brilliant challenge week reported, turns out to be far more interesting.

Your instructions are pretty simple: Go somewhere public and stay for a while. It could be a park, a mall, the gas station, a café, the hallway at work or school. Once you get there, hang out. Watch people, or birds, or anything that strikes you. No need to sit on a park bench for an hour. It can be as short as you like. If you really feel uncomfortable lingering in a spot to observe, then you can do this exercise while walking. But it should have a different quality than Challenge Two—to keep your devices out of sight while in motion. Here I'm asking you to pause and imagine what a single person is thinking, or zoom in on an un-inventable detail. Just make one small observation you might have missed if your nose were glued to a screen. I'm asking you to notice—because noticing is the first step in creating.

I love this story from Nisha Ahamed, an art student, because it shows how the simple act of noticing can lead to intellectual connections, creative acts, and personal insight. You can also see how observations can happen anywhere, since Nisha wasn't in a new or public place but right in her own home, looking at something twenty years old:

"During the challenge, I started looking at things much more closely, and 'saw' for the first time a framed postcard I had on my wall at home," Nisha wrote. "I got it more than twenty years ago at a museum in Canada, and always found it really compelling. I had it taped up above my desk in college, and have displayed it in some way in all the places I have lived since then." Describing the image as a "haunting painting of an old First Nations man," the descendants of Canada's original inhabitants, Nisha said, "In looking at it again, I became curious about the artist, the subject, and the story behind the painting." She took the postcard out of the frame and read the painting's title, *Old Mike*. But the artist's name was faded.

After some research, Nisha discovered the artist was Arthur Shilling, a Canadian Ojibway man, who died in 1985 at the age of forty-four. This inspired her to order a book, *The Ojibway Dream*, a series of Shilling's paintings of his Ojibway people, which included accompanying text written by the artist right before his death.

"I have been mulling over his technique and how with minimal detail, he can create such expressive portraits," Nisha wrote. "So this morning, when I got to work, before I started checking my e-mails, I just sat quietly for a few minutes, which I have been trying to do every day, as a result of the B & B Project. I still had Arthur Shilling and his portraits in my subconscious, and picked up a pen and Post-it pad, and tried to imagine breaking a face into simple broad strokes, the way Shilling did, and came up with a sketch. . . . I've never tried to draw a face before, and it's no Shilling, of course, but it is certainly more than I ever thought of doing, or thought I could do."

Nisha's story encapsulates everything that Bored and Brilliant is supposed to be about: letting your mind wander wherever it wants to go; seeing old things in a new way; making new connections; taking micro risks; and surprising yourself.

My own small observation keeps on giving. I now notice how often people are walking down the sidewalk and talking to themselves, like an eleven-year-old girl I saw walking home, having an animated conversation with no one, her mouth going, only some words actually coming out aloud. I suspect she was practicing how she was going to start a conversation with the cool girls at the playground the next day, rehearsing her facial expression, the funny joke her dad prepped her with. Or this: I ran out of the studio to grab a salad at lunchtime and saw an older woman, black hair scraped up into a bun. I don't think she even knew she was doing it, walking while lifting her eyebrows up and down and making O's with her mouth. I can only guess that she was reenacting and processing a surprise phone call she'd just received from the man she'd been flirting with online. He'd finally decided to book a ticket from London and actually come see her. Or so I imagined.

CHALLENGE UPGRADE

Instead of only noticing, make the act a little more *active* by recording what you observe. Don't judge your observations, or yourself. Just put down whatever you see in whatever way you see fit. In her essay "On Keeping a Notebook," the writer Joan Didion described her notes as "bits of the mind's string too short to use, an indiscriminate and erratic assemblage with meaning only for its maker." Writer Gary Shteyngart, another notebook fan, said, "You need to be what Saul Bellow called the great Noticer. Notice everything around you." Shteyngart recalled that, before the days of the iPhone, he would take a cab downtown, stare out the window, and notice a thousand things. When he got home, he, too, would jot them all down. "Now I can't notice anything because I am tweeting," he half joked, adding, "What is really being lost for someone like me is the ability to be present in the world."

If you choose to do this challenge upgrade, I suggest using a real notebook as opposed to your phone. There's a difference to writing on paper versus digitally. (Yes, there are scientific studies on it.) You don't have to be a writer to experience the artistic effects. The futurist Rita King guarantees that a day of jotting down the un-inventable details will "make your brain feel different, better, more creative."

Notes on Challenge Six

"I noticed how much sunlight there is left in the sky at 5:45 P.M., so even though I'm surrounded by snow, the days are getting longer."

—Brian

"I looked across the way and there was a man sitting at a table all by himself. He grabbed his fish and chips with one hand, and pulled a pepper grinder out of his pocket. He ground some pepper on his fish and chips and put it back into his pocket. I like to imagine that he walks around with his pepper shaker in his bag just on the off chance that he needs it for whatever food he might be eating."

—Lisa

"I was sitting in a café and I noticed that the screen of my iPhone kept blinking. And when I looked I realized it was actually a reflection of birds flying I was seeing on my screen. I thought it was pretty cool."

—Valeria

8

Wander Away

We always like to do things that we like but, because of that, we never change. In un- known territory and in things you don't like, things you fear—that is where you get change.

—Marina Abramović

In 2010, the performance artist Marina Abramović broke attendance records for the Museum of Modern Art when 850,000 people came to see her retrospective, many of them lining up all night for a chance to participate in a piece called *The Artist Is Present*.

Most of us these days, even art lovers, choose binge-watching Netflix with ready access to snacks and a comfy couch over museum exhibi- tions. So what inspired such passion that folks spent all night on New York sidewalks, waiting to gain entrance? Something entrancing. Under bright klieg lights, Abramović offered to sit in a straight-backed chair for seven hours a day, six days a week, staring into the eyes of anyone seated across from her, for as long as they wanted.

Fourteen hundred people took Abramović up on her invitation. Some were famous, like Lou Reed, James Franco, Sharon Stone, Jemima Kirke, and Björk. Some stayed for only a minute. A few others sat for an entire day. A club quickly formed of people who had sat with Abramović more than ten times. Many were so deeply moved, they wept. The artist described the essence of the work's transcendence.

"I give people a space to simply sit in silence and communicate with me deeply but nonverbally," she told *The Observer*. "I did almost nothing, but they take this religious experience from it. Art had lost that power, but for a while MoMA was like Lourdes."

Abramović is all about pushing herself—and the people around her—to the limit, seeing how far she (and they) can and will go, to get in touch with humanity, good and bad. At its core, her goal is to make her audience and herself more present in time and space. To that end, many of her endeavors—such as her Abramović Method, a series of purposeful exercises including simply walking slowly through a room—are aimed at counteracting "the rushed pace of day-to-day living."

In her 2015 show *Goldberg*, pianist Igor Levit performed Bach's *Goldberg Variations* inside the large and cavernous New York Armory. It was also an exercise in limiting contemporary distractions—in the severest way. Every night, for nearly two weeks, when audience members showed up, they were handed a key to an assigned locker in which they were to place their watch, telephone, computer, or any other device. Then they walked inside the armory itself and lay on one of the hundreds of white cloth deck chairs semicircling a stage. On each chair was a pair of noise-canceling headphones. When a single gong rang out, the audience put on the headphones and, for the next thirty minutes, sat in stark silence, with nothing happening. No gadgets, no distractions. Just dimmed lights and perfect strangers surrounding you. (And, yes, the sound of hearing your own breathing was almost deafening, like scuba diving for the first time, and with some of the claustrophobia, too.)

"Of course, I am expecting the first fifteen minutes to be hell for most of the people because they're not used to actually just being there with themselves," Abramović told me at the time of the show. "When you put on the headphones, you even hear your heartbeat. You are more aware of yourself than ever. But after ten or fifteen minutes, somehow you start breathing more slowly. The mind becomes quiet. You start feeling the benefit. But you have to go through the fifteen minutes to pass through this other part."

Silence would help the audience get prepared mentally, physically, and spiritually to receive *Goldberg* instead of the usual rushing to a concert by taxi or subway, answering your last phone call right before you walk into the music hall, and checking your Twitter feed one last time before the lights go down. Usually, Abramović said, "You're not ready to hear anything."

A few months before staging *Goldberg*, she had read an article in *The New York Times* about a Mahler concert where audience members texted, talked to each other, and even let their phones ring. Abramović was horrified. "If Igor has enormous discipline to learn by heart the *Goldberg Variations*, eighty-six minutes of music, and play in the most incredible magic way," she said, "we can have discipline to honor this."

Beyond respect for the musician, however, was a desire to give audience members a "completely fresh experience" that went deeper than Levit's virtuosic playing. As Zachary Woolf wrote in his review of *Goldberg* for *The New York Times*, the performance was masterful, "But I kept returning to that luxuriously quiet half-hour prelude. Never before had I considered silence as a commodity."

The modern world we live in is one of constant distractions, Abramović argues. And one in which having the patience to connect to yourself is becoming increasingly difficult. Returning to the moment when audience members have to give away their watches and phones, she said, "You think that you are disconnected. But the question is, what are you disconnected from? You're actually constantly disconnected from yourself by having all of these things."

For Abramović, who believes in approaching the world with an "absolutely open heart and curiosity," "the only way for us to survive is to go back to simplicity."

I might not put it quite so dramatically as Abramović. (When it comes to drama in general, no one can match her.) But, yes, this is what the Bored and Brilliant Project is all about: losing a little of the tools that give us a lot in the way of information, immediate productivity, and assurance in order to regain some of the simplicity and wonder that lead to deeper creativity, insight, and calm.

Silencing our devices, however, is really just the beginning of the process. As Svetlana Alexievich said, through an interpreter, in her acceptance of the 2015 Nobel Prize in Literature, "Freedom is not an instantaneous holiday, as we once dreamed. It is a road, a long road." While the heroic Belarusian nonfiction writer was talking about humanity in the wake of fallen totalitarian regimes and not what to do with yourself when you've deleted *Candy Crush*, there is a parallel, and the comparison is not as flip as it might sound.

Embracing boredom requires us to make choices about how we spend our time. And in order not to fall right back into filling a day up or downright wasting it, we need to give ourselves permission to say no to the cult of busyness. As Abramović challenged the *Goldberg* audience, we must ask what we're afraid of finding when we let our minds wander and reconnect with ourselves. Easier said than done; using concrete tools, like Abramović's methodologies, can be the fastest way to get reaccustomed to more mind-wandering and reconnecting.

But we aren't all avant-garde artists or the well-heeled patrons who can afford to get tickets to an event like *Goldberg*. What tools are easily available to all of us? As we discussed in the previous chapter, actively observing the world around you is one way to get into this mode. Futurist Rita King, who described the "un-inventable details" in chapter 7, puts this process at the core of her creativity. King gets *paid* to think up plausible scenarios no one else can imagine. Movie studios hire her when they have a film that is set in the future and they want it to look fanciful and far-out, but still believable. Like, in a century or two from now, what will a town or village look like? What will the citizens of that future town or village be doing on a daily basis? Corporations also hire King to predict their consumers' habits decades from now.

Ironically, King says the secret to putting herself into the minds of people who live in the future is "being radically present"—something she achieves by recording the "little things that make an environment unique to itself." That could be anything from a snippet of dialogue overheard in a restaurant to the color of someone's sweater to the way a bird flies across the sky. "I don't have a crystal ball, even though I'm a professional futurist," King said. "But I have been keeping notebooks for my entire life, and I write down what I see."

The biggest ideas start with the tiniest observation, according to King. One of those un-inventable details can snowball into a full-on imaginative thought that gets the observer to completely "re-see" his surroundings. The beauty of this process is that you don't need to worry about the big ideas, just the tiny observations. Through mind-wandering, your brain will take care of the rest.

Mind-Wandering versus Mindfulness

A quick word on the difference and relationship between mind-wandering and mindfulness and their respective benefits. Meditation and mindfulness have become popular because of their potential to tame unproductive thoughts that get ramped up with information overload. Techniques involving focusing on the breath and clearing the mind can help people feel more positive, calm, and able to regulate emotion. Despite its scientifically proven benefits, meditation might also dampen your creativity.

In a 2011 fMRI study, Yale's Dr. Judson Brewer found that the default mode network was deactivated in experienced meditators. Brewer—who started meditating in medical school as a way to manage stress and is now a recognized expert in mindfulness training for addiction treatment—performed brain scans on subjects using three types of mindfulness meditation techniques. (They included concentrating on breathing, loving-kindness through repetition of a phrase, and choiceless awareness, when the subject focuses on whatever object comes to mind. For all three the study stated, "Our findings demonstrate differences in the default-mode network that are consistent with decreased mind-wandering.")

This poses a conundrum. Mindfulness meditation, a stress-reliever, turns off the region of the brain involved in daydreaming. That's where our most original ideas come from, and yet all that mental jumping around done in the brain's default mode network can pile onto that awful scatterbrained or monkey-mind feeling. Or it can be a fertile breeding ground for negative ruminating thoughts. The Imagination Institute's Scott Barry Kaufman, who has contemplated the problematic paradoxes of mindfulness versus mind-wandering, says the two can be reconciled "by understanding that there are different ways you can be mindful, and there are different things you can be mindful of."

According to Kaufman, not all meditation practices are equal. Mindfulness exercises that encourage you to let go of all thoughts (returning to the breath, and so forth) are uncreative. (Certainly, these forms are incredibly valuable for many people looking for ways to reduce anxiety. If that is your goal, of course you should continue your practice.) But "open-monitoring meditation," exercises that encourage you to notice experiences, can jump-start mind-wandering. "Active open-minded awareness meditation, where you're nonjudgmentally open to any thoughts that arise as well as anything in your environment," he said. "That's the form of mindfulness most conducive to creativity."

Focus in the Age of Distraction

Greg McKeown has made an entire business out of helping people figure out how they should spend their time. His leadership training company, This, Inc., works with high-level executives from Google, LinkedIn, and Pixar, helping them hone the precepts laid out in his bestselling book *Essentialism: The Disciplined Pursuit of Less*.

McKeown's method is geared toward figuring out what matters most to you and "designing a life" around that thing. He breaks the process down into three basic steps, the first of which is "to create space in our lives to figure out what is essential." Step two is to "eliminate all the nonessential activities." The third and last is to reallocate the resources that have been freed up and invest them in pursuing those things we've decided matter most to us.

I try to do "essentialism" every August—which I think of as my reset month—but I wondered if most people already feel too overwhelmed to ask themselves (every once in a while, much less every day) if what they *are* doing is the most important thing they *should* be doing and if that thing is getting them closer to their broader goal.

McKeown says that, yes, people are stretched too thin and they feel "busy but not productive" precisely because they are making default decisions. Sometimes these are psychological defaults, such as a habit of saying yes to all work or home requests because you worry about being disliked if you ever said no. But technology, as we've seen, continues to play a greater role in how we run our lives. Presented with so many choices every day, many of us don't have the energy to actually make them and leave the deciding to our devices.

"Technology makes a great servant but a poor master," McKeown said. "There are so many ways of consuming technology that are not consistent with what you're trying to do." And lest you think that the big-time consultant who speaks to companies all over the world about how to focus on the important doesn't get caught up in the technology time-suck himself . . . "There are endless times where I find myself isolated doing e-mail or whatever that doesn't need to be done," he said. "I wonder if my tombstone might read, 'He checked e-mail.'" (If that's McKeown's tombstone, mine would definitely read, "She clicked links and saved lots of articles to read at another time. And then never actually read them.")

This businessperson, speaker, author, and father of four ("which is not very essentialist of me," McKeown admitted) struggles with daily digital tasks just as the rest of us do. Interestingly, he believes his biggest hurdle isn't information overload but rather "opinion overload." He isn't anti–social media per se, "but we have to learn to live in a world where anyone can have an opinion about anything you're doing. Regardless of whether they have any information or you value their opinion." Internet trolls, Twitter bullies, and Facebook aggression—it's enough to make even an inspirational entrepreneur's head spin. "By the time I've woken up in the morning," McKeown said, "I can't remember what was important to me anymore."

So far technology is the greatest distraction of all time, which is precisely why McKeown argues we have to increase our awareness of and ability to make choices about how we use it. "Technology is this enabler of something," he said, "but not if we don't know what the something is."

That gets us back to essentialism or prioritizing, which became one of McKeown's favorite words while he was doing research for his book and discovered that "priority" first came into the English language in the 1400s and the concept was *singular*. "The very first or prior thing. Sensibly, for the next five hundred years, it stayed singular," he said. It wasn't until the Industrial Revolution, when people had to deal with multiple simultaneous activities (taking care of the children while running the washing machine and vacuuming), that the noun was used plurally, irrevocably changing the original concept. "How can we have very many first, before-all-the-things things?" McKeown asked. "Of course we can't."

And yet, we try. Never more so than right now.

It drives McKeown crazy whenever priorities proliferate—even on the radio. Case in point, he had his car radio tuned to NPR (what else?), which was airing an interview with a new mayor who, in response to a question about his top three priorities, said he had two dozen priorities, none more or less important than the other. McKeown wanted to scream, "Nooooo!" "It was like watching a bad movie, for a second time, in slow motion," he said. "We've seen the results before—if you try to do a bit of everything, you're going to make a millimeter of progress in a million directions." The mayor's city has real challenges requiring trade-offs and hard decisions about where to put resources that can ultimately make the biggest difference. Think of this city as a metaphor for pretty much everyone's life.

McKeown realizes turning to essentialism is a "big shift in mind-set" for most of us. But he insists that "almost everything is nonessential and a few things are incredibly valuable. As soon as you have that under-standing, it becomes nature, intuitive, to say, 'I'm going to spend the time figuring that out.'"

The process begins, McKeown said, with holding a "personal off-site" (ideally every ninety days). Modeled on a retreat he holds for senior cor-porate leaders in Napa Valley, this assignment can be done by anyone anywhere, he said. (In fact, This, Inc. launched a "huge social experi-ment" by inviting the whole city of L.A. to hold a virtual personal off-site.) The purpose of the off-site is to ask yourself questions about what's important in your life. Using those answers, you then create a one-page life design in the form of a grid where you identify your top five roles. He recommends people do the exercises in pencil so that the steps to get to the goals can keep evolving through what he calls the "grid glance." "Every morning the first thing you do, before the phone, is reach for the grid and make tiny microadjustments," he said. "Three seconds of just glancing over it . . . the cumulative effect of that can be life changing."

The thrust of essentialism is giving yourself the time and space to figure out what's important to you and then consistently checking in with yourself to make sure you take the steps to achieve your original goals. The process is constant, but McKeown says the results are worth the vigilance. He has story after story of people who made huge changes. One woman managed to negotiate five days off for her wedding, after never negotiating with management before. She even pushed back when her boss tried to renege on the deal at the last minute and was so proud of her new gumption that she wrote the incident into her vows! "People have permission to do not just what everyone else is doing," McKeown said.

While the work of essentialism, or any method of focusing ourselves, can seem like yet more work, even drudgery, McKeown argues that it's the opposite. "It's delight and surprise. It is magic," he said. Words like "routine" get a bad rap, but there's nothing inherently bad about a routine—unless your routine is filled with things you hate doing.

Citing the example of his business partner, Shawn Vanderhoven, McKeown describes how Vanderhoven labeled one of his major roles as "playful father" during his personal off-site. To fulfill that essential role, Vanderhoven adjusted his weekly schedule to include time spent surfing with his three boys. They now have a set afternoon to be in the water and just be together, having fun.

Sounds so simple, right? Sigh. If you've ever tried to alter the routines in your life, you know how deceptively hard it can be. McKeown's advice: Go for the "tiny changes." "You can start to bend the routine toward the things that are essential. It can be done," he said. "But you have to start very small and be gentle with yourself. Enjoy the journey. Don't beat yourself up if you get caught up in the trivial many rather than the vital few."

I decided that to be a "present mother," I needed to do school pickup on Fridays. From my first day at WNYC, I blocked that afternoon in my schedule. It's not always convenient, but I'll sacrifice those hours with my kids at the playground only for the most vital interview or meeting.

Space Cadets Rule

Grid glances aren't the only way to work on your goals. Boredom, or more specifically, mind-wandering, encourages autobiographical planning—which is a fancy, scientific way of describing how our mind thinks through and plans the steps we need to take to reach our personal goals and organize our lives over extended periods of time.

"The lives of our species are very complicated, and they're not always lived in the moment," said the University of York's Jonathan Smallwood. "We spend a lot of our time in a moment that is connected to both moments in the past and moments in the future."

Smallwood's 2011 study on the content of mind-wandering found the cognitive activity to be "predominantly future-focused," and "frequently involves autobiographical planning." Those are "useful to the individual as they navigate through their daily lives," the study stated.

The professor of cognitive neuroscience used an example close to home to illustrate his point: school. "Every moment of your school life, you're usually confronted with the choice between studying or partying," he said. "Obviously, the nice thing to do might be to party, because it's good fun. . . . But in the long run, what you need to do is study because that opens opportunities in the future, might get you better jobs and perhaps more stable relationships." Spoken like a true professor.

Whether you're a PhD candidate or professional Ping-Pong player, success involves measuring the pros and cons and then making a plan of action. The alternative is either long hours of couch-bound inertia or feeling trapped in a job or situation that you can't even remember how you got into. "The day-dreaming state is all about helping people organize themselves so that they can achieve things that are complicated because they take a lot of time to do," Smallwood said.

Can Mindfulness Be a Force for Creativity?

Chade-Meng Tan took a page right out of the essentialism handbook when he retired from his job at Google in 2015.

It wasn't just because the engineer is a two-time *New York Times* bestselling author or the cochair of One Billion Acts of Peace, which has received eight nominations for the Nobel Peace Prize. Or that he's also the chairman of the Search Inside Yourself Leadership Institute, an organization that promotes mindfulness and emotional intelligence worldwide.

"The most direct impetus for me when I decided to retire from Google was to spend more time in my meditation," said Tan, who decided he wanted to meditate as much as a professional musician practices or a pro athlete trains. He decided on three hours a day—for forty days in a row.

"Then my e-mails started piling up and my to-do list started piling up," he said. "That's why I retired: not to build technology but just to become a full-time mental athlete."

We need to back up a little bit. Before he became a mindfulness star, Tan was a software engineer at Google, which he joined in 2000 as Employee No. 107. He had a background in artificial intelligence and cultivating the mind. His conversion to meditation occurred around his twenty-first birthday. Before that, he said, "I was miserable. I had to learn to be happy." (He blames his negative state on losing "the genetic lottery.") His lessons in happiness began when he attended a talk by a Tibetan Buddhist nun and instantly decided to learn meditation.

That wasn't Tan's last epiphany. He had another one in 2003 while taking a walk outside the Google building and "letting his mind wander." "Suddenly I knew what I wanted to do for the rest of my life, which was to create the conditions for world peace in my lifetime," he said. Typical Google employee thinking small. That's what a walk and some mind-wandering will get you.

For Tan, in order to create those conditions for peace, there needed to be a way to "scale inner peace and joy and compassion worldwide." He set about solving the world's problems the way any top engineer would. He created a program that had the end goal of inner transformation, but with a more relatable incentive: personal success. What better way to appeal to the type-A achievers surrounding him at Google headquarters in Silicon Valley? He could teach them to be better at their jobs but also give them the sneaky side effects of peace, joy, and compassion. Tan made sure to develop a curriculum for his colleagues that was thoroughly backed by science, was precise in its terminology, and had an application in the business world (yes, even love and kindness). He called his program Search Inside Yourself—a jokey reference to the search engine company's original mission.

While today mindfulness is as normal as Starbucks, back then, Tan said, "It was weird." The class took a while to catch on, but word of mouth spread, and soon SIY became one of the most popular classes of the hundreds offered at Google.

Many employees called Tan's curriculum "life changing." That sounds more like the hyperbolic talk of a New Age spiritualist rather than hard-core engineers. But Tan says learning meditation can change many aspects of one's life, just as getting physically fit can improve a wide range of health issues, from sleep to confidence. "Mindfulness and meditation," he said, "are training for the mind."

It wasn't just an internal shift that these Google employees experienced. Those who took Tan's class saw tangible benefits that they directly attributed to their new mind-calming capabilities. Engineers solved intractable problems and earned promotions. Managers got to the root of and fixed bad working relationships. Spouses reported that their partners were lighter—happier.

Perhaps that's what makes Tan's last title at Google, Jolly Good Fellow, so appropriate—even though, he said, it "started as a joke, like most things in my life."

A little Google history and inside info: The highest-ranking engineer at the company earns the title Google Fellow. One day Tan joked, "Why be a Google Fellow when you can be a Jolly Good Fellow?" Everybody laughed, which in Tan's philosophy meant he was on the right track. So he took the liberty of having this newly coined job title printed on his official business card, with the phrase "which nobody can deny" in parenthesis, and without telling human resources. HR turned out to have a sense of humor and let him keep the title. It wound up in a story in *The New York Times* and Tan "got stuck with it."

Even though he's left Google, Tan is still a jolly good fellow, spreading mindfulness by emphasizing "ease and joy." Whether it's in his seminars or his books, *Search Inside Yourself* and *Joy on Demand*, he puts forward an unintimidating and, frankly, unmysterious approach to meditation. Most people are intimidated by mindfulness, because "they come to the first class and then the teacher, usually somebody without hair, says, 'Now let's sit for the next hour.' What? An hour? Are you kidding me?"

In *Joy on Demand*, the first exercise is a single breath. "One in breath, one out breath, taken with total but gentle attention," he said. "And when people do that, already they feel better."

That's all it takes, according to Tan, to activate the relaxation response, which lowers the heart rate and loosens muscles. "If you practice with intensity, just a very short amount of practice can bring you a lot of benefit," he said. "That is what allows beginners to have very short practices that are immediately effective."

TAN'S TEN-SECOND MEDITATION PRACTICE

Here's a brief exercise Tan crafted to prove that meditation can be as quick and useful as a Google search. This one is geared to upping your kindness quotient (which Tan says makes you happier).

1. Bring a person into your mind, preferably someone you care about.
2. Think *I wish for this person to be happy.*
3. Maintain the thought for three breaths, in and out.
4. Do this every day to turn your wish for other people's happiness into a habit . . . that will bring you happiness, too.

Meditating might make us kinder and more joyful—but what about the claims that it's not conducive to creativity? Tan mentioned he has lots of good ideas and insights while meditating. Is the branding off-message with meditating or what?

The answer, according to Tan, is yes and no.

"Mindfulness is not a cognitive faculty, like mind-wandering," he said. "Mindfulness is an attention faculty. Initially it's simply about stabilizing your attention."

Tan is referring to the first step in meditation: learning to train your attention by focusing it fully on the breath. In a way, this is the warm-up for your mental muscles before they get whipped into shape for the big game. Simple breathing techniques—such as saying "one" every time you breathe out—stabilize our attention and clear out everything else. "Eventually, to the mind, there's nothing but the breath," Tan said. "That frame of mind is very calm, but it's not conducive to creativity."

Tan explained that when we calm down, thinking becomes slower, but at this point, it doesn't completely stop. In this state, thoughts become slower . . . and clearer. Because they are slower, they are easier to capture, like fish moving slowly in cold waters. "The clarity of seeing the mind improves," Tan said, "and in that state, that's when for me the mind is most creative." Relaxed yet alert, "ideas just start popping up."

Because he is deeply experienced in mindfulness, Tan can choose another mode of meditation known as "open attention" when he wants to promote creativity rather than relaxation. "I apply moment-to-moment nonjudging attention," he said. "However, this time I allow thoughts to come and go as they wish. And so I just become the observer, observing a stream of thoughts. And that mind is very conducive to creativity."

If you think being able to watch your thoughts sail by without feeling guilty, anxious, or insecure is the Zen version of the Holy Grail, you're almost right. But wait, there's more. As the mind grows calmer and calmer in this attention-ability game, ultimately, you can choose to turn it off altogether. "You can get into a state where there's no thought at all," said Tan, who recalled having a lunch with the famed spirituality writer Eckhart Tolle. The author of *The Power of Now*, which has sold millions of copies and been translated into thirty-three languages, told Tan, "My biggest achievement in my life is whenever I don't want to think, I don't have to think."

That's the biggest achievement for the man who cohosted a set of webinars with Oprah Winfrey that have been viewed by more than thirty-five million people? Isn't switching our brains off what most of us do when we turn on the Internet, video games, or social media?

"That distracts our brains," Tan corrected me. "It doesn't switch off."

Don't misunderstand Tan. Despite his retirement from Google, he isn't technologically celibate. The former engineer is a huge fan of *Pokémon Go*. "I play every day," he said. "I'm level twenty-five. I'm fairly good at it. My wife is level twenty-six."

Tan's distinction between positive and negative technological use is all about the intention. Because of his meditation practice, his mind is clear enough to have insight into his behavior. *Pokémon Go* gets him out of the house every day as he runs around the park, finding characters. "I notice what it does for me and know that that's why I'm doing it," he said. "So I do it with eyes open."

When you're unconscious, that's when bad things happen. "I call it junk surfing," he said. "Spending hours on Facebook not doing anything, consuming the information equivalent of junk food."

In order to consume information, you need to pay attention, or as Tan put it, "The currency of information is attention." An overabundance of information, through a mindless consumption of all that junk information, will lead to a poverty of attention.

The first step to that devolution, according to Tan, is realizing it's happening. "The solution is insight and awareness and to some degree mastery over the mind," he said. "Maybe you're still on Facebook all day, but now you do it consciously. You do it deliberately."

CHALLENGE SEVEN:
The Bored and Brilliant Challenge

This seventh and final step is the culmination of the first six. You've taken a good hard look at your digital habits, made strides in using tech purposefully, abstained from photo taking, and considered life beyond the screen. Now it's time to put everything together, and get bored—really bored—and in so doing, discover a new level of introspection, creativity, discovery, and courage.

Here are the instructions for this challenge:

Step I: Identify an aspect of your life that you've been confused by, avoiding, or downright terrified to think about. It could be something as large and consequential as figuring out a new career path, or something a lot smaller, like why you never plan vacations and just where you'd go if you did take one. Perhaps you'd just like to come up with a new organizational system for the dry goods in your kitchen cabinets. The point is to name the issue that, whenever you think about solving it, you always seem to end up on Facebook instead.

Step II: Set aside thirty minutes where you'll be completely free from distraction—no kids in the other room or friends dropping by for a quick visit. Store away your phone, tablet, laptop, or any other digital device. Put a generous pot of water on the stove and watch it come to a boil. If you don't have a stove or pot, find a small piece of paper and write "1,0,1,0" as small as you can until the paper is full.

Step III: Immediately after you've completed Step II, and are mind-numbingly bored, sit down with a pen and pad and put your mind to the task of solving the problem identified in Step I. Just as with Dr. Sandi Mann's experiment involving the phone book and paper cups, you will bring new creativity and focus to whatever subject you've chosen. If you are a visual person and the problem you've set out to solve requires drawing (a new bedroom layout, perhaps), go ahead and draw. If you are a list-maker, make a list. The point is to come up with new ideas and get them down on paper. Don't worry about executing the plan just yet—that will come in time. Right now, the goal is to use boredom to unlock a brilliant solution to your problem.

Notes on Challenge Seven

"I posed a serious knotty question—how do I recalibrate or completely rework the tail end of my working life? And made quite a good beginning list."

—Andrew

"I'd really like to eliminate the piles of paper around my house. In my kitchen alone I have two junk drawers that are overfilled, a pile on the counter of random important papers and a pile on my kitchen table of kid-related important papers. This doesn't even begin to touch the amount of paper stacks in my home office. I want to end the paper! I had to do the "1,0" option and I have to say, this is definitely the most I've written this year . . . maybe the most I've handwritten anything since grad school. But I came up with solutions: I need to get off mailing lists and go paperless wherever I can. I need a specific bag in my closet that is my "item to return bag" from online shopping (so the box doesn't sit out somewhere). I need a shredder. I need to get the app that saves your kid's art pieces and makes it into a book because I currently have every piece of preschool for the last two years. It must go. I need to get a place to store physical printed-out pictures and it needs to be outside of my kitchen junk drawers. Now . . . when do I find the time to actually put this plan [in]to action?"

—Matilde

"Watching the water boil calmed me down and put me in a bit of [a] trance. I focused on the tiny bubbles popping up from the bottom of the pot. My challenge was a big scary question: Do I want to be a mother? What I came up with is that motherhood is a process. It's not an easy yes-or-no answer, because there are many forms of motherhood. Maybe I want to be a mom, but adopt? Maybe I'm happy being a very involved auntie to the children of family and friends? Maybe I'm okay with being a mom to a pet or two? In the end, I reminded myself that I need to be more patient. I live by Rilke's "live the questions now," so living these questions sometimes means watching a pot of water come to a boil. Maybe I don't have the answers now, but the water boiling exercise demonstrates that the same inputs get the same outputs. So maybe that's just enough of a nudge to change something small to help me unravel this really big 'mother' of a question."

—Cassie

9

You Are Brilliant

Nobody can give you wiser advice than yourself.

—Cicero

When we at *Note to Self* first set out on this grand experiment called Bored and Brilliant, I'm not sure we knew exactly what we were looking for or what success would truly look like. There was a vague notion of bringing back some of the quiet, reflective time that so many of us feel like our gadgets have disrupted. And we assumed that, through our series of somewhat speculative challenges, we'd give our audience a taste of living life with a deeper consideration of how technology fits into it. Maybe a few of those people would even gain the added benefit of jump-starting their creativity, as I had.

The response was more than we ever imagined. Thousands more people signed up than we expected. People of all ages, from all places, with all perspectives. And their enthusiasm was far greater than we anticipated—it seemed we weren't the only ones with this unsettling desire to put our devices in perspective. But, most surprising, the changes they accomplished through our simple set of challenges were far more acute and thought provoking than we knew.

We heard from teenagers who suddenly found schoolwork easier to understand, authors who completed manuscripts, employees who felt less burnout, and entrepreneurs who had time to think through issues that had been plaguing them and their businesses. Most of all, people felt, as Carter from Brooklyn did, "as if awakening from an extended mental hibernation." And they changed their relationships to their phones, like Zoe from Chicago, who said, "My phone feels more inert, less precious. It's a tool again, not a confidant or loved one."

Because this was an experiment revolving around technology, we also have more than just anecdotal evidence of behavioral shifts. We also have data.

When we started this project, our group was spending about two hours a day on their phones. Over the course of that inaugural challenge week, they checked their phones fewer times each day and spent fewer minutes on their phone. Those who said gaming was one of their top three phone activities dropped the most time on their phones, with twenty fewer minutes of use per day. But the group's average decrease was six fewer minutes of use and one less pickup per day.

Bored and Brilliant by the Numbers

A general note on these stats: they are all correlations and not causations—we don't know what motivated each individual's behavior, whether it was the Bored and Brilliant challenges, app reminders, or anything else. That said, here's how the first group fared.

Total participants: 20,000.

Percentage of females to male: 75 to 25.
Average age: 36.
About 40 percent of the participants had children.
The average decrease in phone use was six fewer minutes and one less pickup each day than the starting baseline.
Over 90 percent of people who filled out our post-challenge survey felt they had cut down on their phone use, either somewhat or a lot.
Ninety percent of the post-challenge survey respondents felt somewhat or very confident that they could change their phone habits. (That's up 10 percent from when respondents took the same survey before the challenge week.)
Gamers made the biggest strides: people who said gaming

was one of the top three activities they did on their
phones managed to drop the most minutes, cutting
down twenty minutes every day.

Before the challenge week, parents averaged more phone
time than nonparents.

Parents dropped ten minutes of phone use per day compared to nonparents, who lost four minutes a day.

The challenge that most people said they would continue in
the future is keeping their phones out of sight
(88 percent, to be precise).

Not surprisingly, the most people—45 percent—also thought
the out-of-sight challenge was the most useful.

Fifty percent of the respondents wanted to stick with deleting
any habit-forming apps, making that the second most
popular challenge after keeping one's phone out of sight
while in transit. The greatest percentage of participants
(32 percent) also found this the most difficult challenge.

I'll be honest, when I got the numbers on our first Bored and Brilliant
challenge group, I was disappointed by them. Especially when I compared them to the powerful stories people were sharing about how this
initiative really changed their lives.

At the start of the project, participants spent about two hours a day on
their phone. They decreased their baseline by only *six* minutes and *one* less
pickup. Those were hardly earth-shattering totals. With numbers so low,
could there be any real meaning here even though people *felt* so strongly?

That's the question I put to Dr. Malia Mason, a cognitive psychologist and associate professor at Columbia Business School who studies
how competing motives shape our judgments, choices, and behaviors.

Calling our initiative "incredibly ambitious," she said, "It's not clear to
me that six minutes isn't meaningful."

She should know. Mason did a study that in some ways was parallel
to ours, in which she surveyed the digital use of 150 Columbia University undergraduates by downloading RescueTime onto their laptops. For
several months, the software tracked when they got on their computers,
when they got off, and how often they switched among activities. "We
were curious how much time people spend on computer-mediated

activities," she said. "But we also are interested in the choices people make with respect to their time and attention."

She was surprised to find that the undergrads ("smart kids who are in a city of endless opportunities and paying lots of money to be here") spent on average twenty-five minutes a day on Facebook. While this seems downright Amish to criticize kids for less than a half hour of Facebook (probably staying in touch with friends and family), the point was these students wanted to spend less time on social media. That's what they *said* was their wish. Plus, Mason said, twenty-five minutes a day adds up to two years of your life.

From her research, Facebook appeared to be the default activity for many of the students. That's not exactly a news flash. As we've discussed, many of us also have the reflex to quickly check social media whenever we get on our computers or phones.

Just as with the Bored and Brilliant Project, Mason wanted to help the participants in her study "make wiser choices and manage their attention more effectively." But in order to fix a problem, you have to figure out the source of the problem in the first place. So she also set about trying to solve that as well.

Her first hypothesis was that students had "an awareness problem."

"People don't realize that their discretionary time is actually quite limited," she said. After sleeping, commuting, eating, and working, Mason estimated they had about four to five hours free every day. She thought maybe those students lost sight of the fact that they have bigger hopes and dreams whenever they get on Facebook. How can you be considering that time is not infinite for anyone on this earth when you are checking likes? Maybe all they needed was a little reminder, some "feedback." Nope. These kids were keenly aware they were wasting their time.

Hypothesis number two was that some people waste more time than others—or what Mason called "a capacity issue." If that turned out to be true, then the solution would be to simply keep those who have trouble paying attention from their computers. But that wasn't it either.

In the end, Mason said, "it appears to be a motivational issue." That's right, people need to *want* to get off Facebook and, even more important, to *believe* they can.

If you look at the problem of tech regulation within that framework,

Mason deemed our Bored and Brilliant experience a huge success because our participants came out of it gaining confidence from their achievements and feeling optimistic about controlling their digital destinies going forward. Indeed, 90 percent of our first survey group reported feeling "somewhat or very confident" that they could alter their future phone-use habits. The number of people who found they had "enough or more than enough time to think" more than doubled after challenge week, leaping from 30 percent to 67 percent.

Participant Eric Greenwald of New York echoed many people's sentiments when he said that, while the time on his phone didn't go down as much as he wanted, "I definitely feel like I'm using it more intentionally. I don't have that guilty gut feeling when I know I'm wasting time on my phone." Eric was pleasantly surprised that when he decided to cut out phone "fluff," he actually did it and saw results. "Maybe I'll have to start giving myself little challenges like this every morning," he said.

"The enthusiasm people have for the initiative, in and of itself, is meaningful," Mason said. It's also a sign of the times. "Many people feel like they're not managing their discretionary time in the way they want to, and that technology is making this problem more difficult," she said. "I mean, who on their deathbed is going to say, 'I only spent two years of my life on Facebook'?"

"It's feasible to get out of this cycle of checking messages, and it doesn't feel too bad!"

—Randy

"I reevaluated how much to take out my phone and use my camera—and whether I really remember things or not because I'm creating a barrier between my reality and my cell phone."

—Nora

"Thank you all so much for inspiring me to learn more about myself. I can and will hold this experience really close to my heart for the rest of my life."

—Christine

We Got Bored

There were so many takeaways from this initiative, but if I had to cite the one I hold most dear, it is this: We sensed that technology was changing us and how we act and think, and with science we proved our intuition was right.

Michael D. Haltenberger, an adjunct lecturer in religion at Hunter College, articulated this sentiment eloquently when he described the motivation behind assigning the Bored and Brilliant challenge to the students in his Religious Experience class. "In the course we discuss the varieties of religious experience (i.e., a transcendent experience that opens us to new perspectives). As we discuss vision quests and drug experiences and the lives of saints and prophets it quickly becomes obvious that the distractions of day-to-day life are a hindrance to unique experience," he wrote. "This has always been the case. Perhaps what is worse now is how easy it is to be distracted. While my students seem to instinctively know that their screen time is affecting their experience of life, few have been bold enough to test it. Bored and Brilliant is the opportunity I've been waiting for in order to force the issue."

The professor hit upon the central point. Bored and Brilliant is a chance to force the issue about something we feel in our gut, and by giving it a structure, we can test whether it is empirically true or not.

The energy and excitement people brought to the initiative were, as Dr. Malia Mason put it, incredibly timely. In our post-challenge data set, Mason was struck by how many respondents indicated that they *wanted* to stop habitually picking up their phones or checking their various devices. That sentiment did not surprise me. We are at a point where it seems no place or person is beyond technology's grip.

With mobile devices and wireless networks becoming ever more accessible through the breaking down of economic and societal barriers, digital technology is imperative to just getting through every day. But there is no denying that these gadgets have a strong effect on us. It's not just teens handing off their Snapchat passwords to friends to use when their parents force them to go on a vacation without Wi-Fi so they can keep collecting points and earning trophy emojis. I also look at someone like my mom, who claims she doesn't like her phone (and, truthfully, really doesn't know how to use most of the apps on it), and yet mentally vanishes into that weird rabbit hole of a blue screen when she checks her messages, just like the rest of us.

Bored and Brilliant even made an impact on those who didn't think technology held this power over them—like my producer. (Or didn't care, like my friend's father, an intelligent and sophisticated man who, after getting his first smartphone at the age of seventy-something, refused to put the thing down—at grandchildren's birthday parties, on the beach, while driving—claiming it was his right, because he was "making up for lost time.") My producer, Alex, really didn't get what we were talking about when I first presented the idea of Bored and Brilliant to him, because he doesn't use his phone or technology all that much. He went through the challenges before we launched the project nonetheless because he's a good producer. The exercises, however, turned out to be incredibly powerful for him, and he realized that he, too, had some changes he wanted to make. (Like so many of us, he had no clue how often he checked his phone.) The challenges brought to light a lot of unconscious behavior that didn't match his self-image.

Whether it's the effect that reading on screens has on attention spans or video game play has on sociability or taking photos has on memory, we are living in an age of self-experimentation. Technology is evolving faster than researchers can study it. Science can't keep up, which is why we need a new interdisciplinary approach, like the one we could offer with Bored and Brilliant. Research now needs to move out of the lab, because life is the new lab.

Get Bored Together

During the first Bored and Brilliant Project, lots of people banded together to do the challenges as a group. At least six different universities incorporated the program into curricula, as Professor Haltenberger did with his religious studies class. Teachers at a smattering of high schools and middle schools across the country also assigned Bored and Brilliant to their students. There was even a preschool classroom that did an adaptation. (The teacher put away her students' favorite flashing toys in favor of earthier materials such as clay and crayons, ignoring their complaints until they started "playing differently.")

We heard about parents roping their teenagers into the challenge, and others recruiting as many as twenty friends to do the week together. At the media and entertainment company Mashable, an entire department went through the challenges as a team.

Turning Bored and Brilliant into a group experience is awesome. Like an exercise program, the week of challenges doesn't take a lot of effort to follow and is really fun. Plus, having other people to inspire you to keep going never hurts.

As with any collective activity, to keep it positive, you need to respect that different members of the group will have different reactions to each challenge.

What's easy or even silly to one person might be soul crushing to another. Don't judge; instead use each exercise as a way to gain new insight into others as you also learn about yourself.

From our own experience at *Note to Self*, challenge week is also a great way to look at how the group works as a whole and find better ways to use technology to communicate with each other. Or not communicate.

In one of my favorite studies, interruption expert Gloria Mark did a Japanese garden study, creating a totally different kind of "prototype designed to help people manage interruptions by broadcasting to colleagues their availability for interruptions." In the experiment, the "garden" was made up of different-colored rocks in a small box of sand, which represented a person's projects and if he or she was at work on them. By arranging the rocks a certain way, each worker could signal wordlessly to colleagues whether she was open to a conversation or needed to be left alone to concentrate. Lovely and Zen idea but, in the end, not a completely successful one. Although the box sat right on a person's desk, Mark found "social agreements are needed as well as a technical solution."

That might explain why when I leave three rakes in the sand of the miniature Japanese garden my team bought me as a gift—meant to symbolize "leave Manoush alone"—it never works.

So what is the "something different that's happening"? Broadly speaking, the gains in experience afforded us by technological advances are immeasurable. We can thank the Internet and our newfound connectivity for a multitude of profound changes, such as:

- new movements toward racial equality in the United States
- the availability of education, no matter location or socio-economic status
- immigrant families, once separated by oceans and the high cost of phone service, staying in touch
- crowd-sourced brain power that scientists have used for everything from redesigning proteins to understanding rare diseases
- the ability for parents in areas with limited access to medical care to receive texts on where to take their children for vaccines
- inexpensive accounting, customer service, sales, and legal tools for small business owners

On a global level, it's safe to say that never before has there been more open access to such a wide range of people, places, and perspectives.

But as we have learned, freedom of access is a misnomer. There are costs. Thoughtful journalism can't survive on digital ads alone, and so newspapers die. Our personal identity and information must be vigilantly protected behind dozens of passwords that we can't remember and may not even be effective. There's no leaving bullies behind on the playground. They exist in every sphere of online social life—and at every age. But perhaps our biggest loss is that of patience. Patience to let someone finish an imperfect sentence; patience to read a dense paragraph not once, twice, but three times to understand an intricate point; patience to let a passing thought that crosses your mind grow into a mediocre concept and only then blossom into an outstanding idea. These things take time. And the one thing our phones can't give us is more hours in the day. Sure, we can be connected to more people and get infinitely more information, but our gadgets don't distinguish between blah-blah communication and that which is worth savoring, thinking about, and then remembering. That is still up to us.

One of my listeners, Julia M. Williams, executive director of the Office of Institutional Research, Planning, and Assessment at the Rose-Hulman Institute of Technology, a college specializing in engineering and other sciences, worries about the impression that phone use makes. She wrote me, "When technical experts don't give their full attention in a meeting or a presentation, they may miss nonverbal cues that can help them interpret the impact of their proposals," she said. "I aspire to have my students become the technical experts who are different from others in the field because they can set down their phones and talk to you."

Like many educators, parents, and employers, Julia finds herself needing to teach a skill—conversation—that she previously took for granted. Talking, listening, eye contact, downtime, responsiveness, and, yes, boredom are all activities that now need to be actively put into practice. It's not that "digital natives" don't feel or know these things; it's just that they don't get prioritized. And so we must name, schedule, and celebrate them. That might feel odd if you've always had these skills, or if you never had them. Nonetheless, we need to value them. And we need to value our alone time. Because all this connectivity can make us feel crazy.

Humans will always find a way to inject irrationality and existential thoughts into even the most inert objects, and technology, which has introduced a whole new realm in which to feel insecure, is no exception. Take Hady Mendez, a listener who works as a lay missionary in Cochabamba, Bolivia. She told us just turning off all the alerts on her phone had a profoundly jarring effect. "It's been hard to go to my phone and not have any notifications waiting for me," she said. "Sometimes I feel, *What, nobody loves me?*" So many people reported feeling the exact same way as Hady, who came to realize that not worrying about those notifications allowed her to *live*. And as someone whose profession is in the spiritual realm, she said, "I need to be more present in the work that I do."

Maybe it's because I'm a mother or someone who likes to imagine she's always in control, but the phone for me has become the "is everything okay?" button. Constantly checking that everyone is fine, happy, and uninjured. This is a constant low-grade vigilance that has always come with being a parent but seems intensified by the phone. The Bored and Brilliant challenge didn't change this neuroticism, but it did allow me to recognize and contemplate it. For example, halfway up the block for a family outing the other night, I realized I had left my phone by the kitchen sink. I decided to force myself *not* to go back and get it. After all, my kids were with me and my husband had his phone. Okay, so this decision wasn't huge or radical, but just leaving my phone behind once in a while and being out in the world without taking a picture of my kids on the subway or compulsively checking my favorite weather app and then refreshing my *New York Times* app to take a quick peek at the headlines are a start. Baby steps. I am still a person in the world even without my phone, even without showing anyone the beautiful sunset I'm witnessing or telling anyone where I am or knowing exactly the fastest way to get somewhere. Because when you don't have control or know everything, you feel a little scared. And when you feel scared, you feel more alive.

It makes me think of Marina Abramović's insight into people's fear of handing over their devices before her musical concert: "You think that you are disconnected. But the question is, what are you disconnected from? You're actually constantly disconnected from yourself by having all of these things."

"I noticed when I stopped using my phone as much, I was more mindful of when my friends used their phones. But also, when I was just standing there they would feel awkward and put their phones away."

—Jamie

"I deleted Twitter, Facebook, Instagram, Tumblr, Snapchat, and Vine from my phone, and it was a kind of embarrassingly emotional experience. At first, it felt weirdly lonely to look at that locked screen with no new notifications on it. But I really like deciding for myself when to think about or access my social networks and not giving my phone the power to decide that for me."

—Rocco

Bored and Beyond

In talking to all the scientists and thinkers for the original initiative and this book, I always asked for their solutions to some of the negative consequences, intended or unintended, of the digital age. I'm a sucker for an expert opinion.

There is a strain of thought that proposes technological solutions to our problems with tech. Tim Berners-Lee, the inventor of the World Wide Web, is working on his own project to give us back control over our data. Malia Mason, our social psychologist at Columbia University's School of Business, played out a plausible scenario of an app designed to keep you on task using the motivational model she believes works best. It goes something like this: You decide you want to run a marathon, and in order to do that, you have to train for an hour a day. You also decide that you want to spend only twenty minutes a day on Facebook. All this information goes into the app, which connects the two activities by interrupting you when you go over your Facebook quota and, if you decide to continue scanning Facebook anyway, shows you the marathon-training time that's being eaten into by social media. Mason's theoretical app is a reminder of what you said you really cared about—that you are making a choice, which has consequences.

There are others, like the Time Well Spent movement's Tristan Harris, who believes that designers and tech leaders need to lead the charge in creating products that "enhance humanity over additional screen time." Harris and the social scientist Joe Edelman are working on a "Hippocratic oath" for software design that includes a code of ethics, ratings system, and certification standards. Soren Gordhamer, the creator of Wisdom 2.0, a popular conference dedicated to the "intersection of wisdom and technology," believes that Silicon Valley's leaders are ready for something like this. "They feel guilty," he told *The Atlantic*. "They are realizing they built this thing that's so addictive."

Maybe. It would be amazing if a real movement grew within the industry to create technology that's better for society. But unless the current business models get completely upended, you'll have to forgive my skepticism. Why change the business model when a company like Snapchat can be valued at twenty-five billion dollars? I wholeheartedly believe consumers should advocate for technology that serves their interests, and those within the industry (and government) should listen. We also need to press regulators and lawmakers to understand the privacy issues and economic inequalities at stake. But in the meantime, we should come out of our *Candy Crush* coma.

We need to listen to our intuition. If you feel bad or anxious or just plain yucky after being online for a couple of hours, there is probably a reason for it—and you can do something about it.

Unlike David Joerg—our game-addicted dad and software developer who built an entire digital Rube Goldberg machine to lock him out of his favorite video game—most of us have to rely on something more simple: self-regulation. We all have it. And it's free of charge! No terms of service to sign either.

I'll admit my powers of self-regulation aren't always what I hoped they'd be. Take my *Two Dots* problem. After I deleted the app, I became that creepy person on the subway who, if I saw someone playing *Two Dots* next to me (which happened pretty regularly), would look over their shoulder, practically panting. I was like a former smoker who went and stood outside with real smokers to take deep breaths and talk about cigarettes. Which is why I didn't put *Two Dots* back on my phone even after Bored and Brilliant ended. Then, about a year later, game designer Jane McGonigal gave me permission to put a new version of *Two Dots* on my phone. I had to travel to Australia for a conference and as a nervous flier was dreading the twenty-two-plus hours in the air. She suggested I use the game as a distraction, to combat my anxiety. For better or worse, it worked.

Because as soon as I touched down back in New York and could have deleted the app, I didn't. I couldn't. I was already at level 82. And I was back in love. But I did do one thing: I filed the game in a virtual folder on my phone labeled PRODUCTIVITY. That way, every time I go to play *Two Dots*, I'm forced to take two extra steps and laugh at my absurd compulsion. Does it stop me? Rarely. I feel sheepish for a moment and then play anyway. But I do try to limit it to five to ten minutes, as McGonigal suggests. This is my DIY version of Mason's theoretical motivational app; making it just a little harder to access something I don't feel great about acts like a speed bump by reminding me, *Manoush, before you get completely sucked in, remember, your game playing is the antithesis of productivity.*

"Before the Bored and Brilliant Project, I calculated that my iPhone usage was about *90 percent* of my waking hours. I was so addicted that I only slept for about four hours a night, and I must have dreamt of my iPhone for at least two of those hours. While wexting, I found myself walking into walls and people. I never texted while driving. Well, except at a stoplight. Sometimes, though, I would pull over to the side of the road for as long as thirty minutes to finish a texting conversation. My wife wasn't too happy about that, because I'd always be late to dinner. But then again I always had my head in the phone during dinner so it didn't make much of a difference anyway. But now, thanks to Bored and Brilliant, my life is so much better. I followed all of its instructions and wow! It really worked! I'm now down to 85 percent of all my waking hours on the phone. I almost don't know what to do with all that recovered time. As a child of the '70s, I have to admit I'm surprised we managed to survive without all that technology. We actually called people on a landline phone. And even worse, we knocked on someone's door to play baseball or some other old-fashioned game. We would go out of the house for hours, and our parents had no idea where we were or how to track us with a thing like Find Friends. If we were running late, we couldn't call and tell them, we're late! My kids refuse to believe that such a world really existed. But then I Netflix an episode of *That '70s Show* and they kind of get the idea. Anyway, thanks again for the newfound time."

—Martin

I don't like it when people call Bored and Brilliant a "digital detox." I'm not against the idea of powering down completely for a specific period of time. Those kinds of breaks are great, when and if you can manage them. But locking your phone away in a drawer doesn't help you develop better habits once that phone is back in your hands.

Bored and Brilliant is about living smarter and better within a digital world. Technology isn't going anywhere, and who would want it to? I love that I have an app on my phone that can tell me the exact subway car I need to be on to get out of the station quickest. What I'm advocating is balancing the way we use technology and making sure, as best we can, that our gadgets align with what we hold dear and true. Yes, we are up against billion-dollar companies and leagues of highly educated and intelligent people paid a lot of money to keep us in a digital feedback loop. But there are actions we can take—and some of them aren't any harder than giving a folder a funny name—to contain the information and stimulation threatening to overwhelm us at every turn.

When talking about this very idea, Michael Pietrus, a psychologist at the Art Institute of Chicago who is married to a digital marketing exec, offered a quotation from the second-century Greek philosopher Epictetus: "If one oversteps the bounds of moderation, the greatest pleasures cease to please." For his part, Pietrus keeps a graphic posted of a little kid behind a tree saying "The Internet will be just fine without you" as a way to remind himself regularly "to be in the world with people and have experiences even if they are challenging."

The hardest stuff is what can also be the most worthwhile, and that's how I feel about finding equilibrium in the digital ecosystem. Like marriage, parenthood, or friendship, our relationship with technology takes constant work.

This dynamic of effort to find the balance is only going to become truer as virtual reality enters into our lives. I picture technology and our most basic human needs as opposite ends of a spectrum. Previously, that spectrum was quite limited. (Think of when the horse and buggy was a big invention. Sure, it was a big deal and changed your sense of distance but not your very sense of existence.) Now the space spanning the two ends of this spectrum is so much greater and growing more vast every day. Either extreme isn't good, and every day we make a myriad of choices that land us usually somewhere in the middle. Should I tweet on a Saturday? Answer this text in a meeting? File this e-mail? Join Instagram? Every day, so many decisions. So many choices. It can feel exhausting, but if the Bored and Brilliant experiment teaches us nothing else, it proves that if you don't make these decisions, there is a company or app or social media site that will make them for you.

There is no sitting this one out.

ACKNOWLEDGMENTS

It took a lot of fascinating people to make a book about boredom.

To my editor, Michael Flamini: We were a match at first sight, thanks to the insightful Jessica Lawrence. So much gratitude to you and the entire enthusiastic and supportive St. Martin's team.

Stuart Krichevsky and Ross Harris at SK Agency, I have awe and appreciation for your guidance and patient phone conversations.

To the researchers, scientists, and scholars who shared their time and discoveries: You inspire me and my audience. Thank you for doing the deep thinking and research needed on these topics.

Truly, I am merely a representative of all my hardworking WNYC colleagues. They were willing to take an inkling of an idea and turn it into a reality none of us predicted. Alex Goldmark and Ariana Tobin were the brilliant co-executors of the original project, and this book could not have happened without them. Jim Schachter, thank you for saying yes, and John Keefe, you and the data news team always make a good idea better and quantifiable.

Many thanks also to Andrew Dunn, Nina Katchadourian, Maria Popova, Kevin Holesh, Jennifer Houlihan Roussel, Mike Hearn, and Ivan Zimmerman. So many other generous and rigorous WNYC colleagues gave their time: to Theodora Kuslan and her team, especially Sahar; John Hersey, your work and your ability to know what our sound should look like is a gift. To Marine, Val, Fiona, Kevin, Alison, and the entire digital team, I so appreciate your efficiency and willingness to experiment. Jacqueline Cincotta, thank you for always having my back. Robin and Rex, thank you for making me coherent.

I need to say a special thank you to the indefatigable Charlie Herman for inducting me into New York Public Radio in the first place. Collin Campbell, our time was brief but pivotal. Jen Poyant, you are my partner in audio and friendship. I can't wait to see what we make next. Especially with Kat Aaron. Joe Plourde, your patience and ear astound. Paula Szuchman, you came up with the name and are so damn good. Jad Abumrad, your blessing on this project made all the McNutt. John Chao, you wrote "book" on a whiteboard and made it so. We did this. Thank you.

Dean Cappello, you and Laura Walker made me an offer I couldn't refuse. Your subsequent faith in my curiosity, patience with creativity, and encouragement to think big guided me to a path I didn't know was available.

Thank you, Kirsten Cluthe, for being my professional sounding board and consistent champion.

To the entire Robin family, especially Lenore and Noel, thank you for your love and generosity and making me one of your own.

To my parents, a decade of weekly and consistent child care made this possible. Your support and generosity over the past forty years have given me a stability that I only now know how much to appreciate.

Armin and Gitta, I can't believe what great siblings you are and that we like each other so much. Gitta, a special thank you to you for editing and talking through ideas when you could have been eating pomme frites in peace. You are my sister.

To my dear Josh. Your tolerance and kindness are true. Nice work on our great life. I love you dearly.

Finally, to the listeners. Your generosity and open minds have taught me so much. Through your stories, I hear the world more clearly. Thank you.

INDEX